Be Alert

BE Books
by Warren Wiersbe

Be Alert

Warren W. Wiersbe

While this book is designed for the reader's personal use and profit, it is also intended for group study. A leader's guide with visual aids (Victor Multiuse Transparency Masters) is available from your local bookstore or from the publisher.

13306

VICTOR BOOKS a division of SP Publications, Inc.
WHEATON, ILLINOIS 60187

Offices also in
Whitby, Ontario, Canada
Amersham-on-the-Hill, Bucks, England

Second printing, 1985

Unless otherwise noted, Scripture quotations are from the *King James Version*. Other quotations are from the *New American Standard Bible* (NASB), © the Lockman Foundation 1960, 1962, 1963, 1968, 1971, 1972, 1973, 1975, 1977; the *Holy Bible, New International Version* (NIV), ©1973, 1978, 1984, International Bible Society. Used by permission of Zondervan Bible Publishers; *The New Testament in Modern English*, Revised Edition (PH), © J.B. Phillips, 1958, 1960, 1972, permission of Macmillan Publishing Co. and Collins Publishers; and *The New Testament: An Expanded Translation* by Kenneth S. Wuest (WUEST). ©1961 by the Wm. B. Eerdmans Publishing Co. Used by permission.

Recommended Dewey Decimal Classification: 227.9
Suggested Subject Headings: BIBLE. N.T. 2 PETER, 2 & 3 JOHN, & JUDE

Library of Congress Catalog Card Number: 84-50147
ISBN: 0-89693-380-6

VICTOR BOOKS
A division of SP Publications, Inc.
Wheaton, Illinois 60187

CONTENTS

Dedicated to
Bob and Betty Kregel

Your friendship has enriched
our lives, and your ministry has
enriched the church around the world.

PREFACE

All is not well in the professing church.

There are dangerous people and dangerous doctrines abroad, and God's people need to be alert.

The church is suffering from a false view of separation as well as a false view of cooperation. Too often we are aiding the enemy and injuring the brotherhood by attitudes and actions that are contrary to God's Word.

Peter, John, and Jude can help us exercise discernment and detect the counterfeits that have secretly entered the church. They can also help us discover the false doctrines that these apostates are teaching, doctrines that today are passing for Christian truth.

In writing this book, I find myself in a position similar to the one Jude described in the opening words of his letter. I would much rather write a book about the blessings of the Christian life, the positive elements of our faith; but when the enemy is abroad, we need a call to arms, not an invitation to a picnic.

"By entertaining of strange persons," said John Flavel, "men sometimes entertain angels unawares; but by entertaining of strange doctrines, many have entertained devils unawares."

It is time to be alert!

Warren W. Wiersbe

A Suggested Outline of 2 Peter

I. EXPLANATION: THE KNOWLEDGE OF CHRIST—1:1-21
   A. The gift of knowledge, 1:1-4
   B. The growth in knowledge, 1:5-11
   C. The ground of knowledge, 1:12-21

II. EXAMINATION: THE FALSE TEACHERS—2:1-22
   A. Their condemnation, 2:1-9
   B. Their character, 2:10-17
   C. Their claims, 2:18-22

III. EXHORTATION: THE TRUE CHRISTIAN—3:1-18
   A. Be mindful, 3:1-7
   B. Be not ignorant, 3:8-10
   C. Be diligent, 3:11-14
   D. Beware, 3:15-18

Knowing and Growing

2 Peter 1:1-11

If anybody in the early church knew the importance of being alert, it was the Apostle Peter. He had a tendency in his early years to feel overconfident when danger was near and to overlook the Master's warnings. He rushed ahead when he should have waited; he slept when he should have prayed; he talked when he should have listened. He was a courageous, but careless, Christian.

But he learned his lesson, and he wants to help us learn it too. In his first epistle, Peter emphasized the grace of God (1 Peter 5:12), but in this second letter, his emphasis is on the knowledge of God. The word *know* or *knowledge* is used at least thirteen times in this short epistle. The word does not mean a mere intellectual understanding of some truth, though that is included. It means a living participation in the truth in the sense that our Lord used it in John 17:3—"This is life eternal, that they might *know* Thee the only true God, and Jesus Christ, whom Thou hast sent" (italics mine).

Peter opened his letter with a description of the Christian life. Before he described the counterfeits, he described the true believers. The best way to detect falsehood is to understand the characteristics of the truth. Peter made three important affirmations about the true Christian life.

The Christian Life Begins with Faith (2 Peter 1:1-4)

Peter called it "like precious faith." It means that our standing with the Lord today is the same as that of the apostles centuries ago. They had no special advantage over us simply because they were privileged to walk with Christ, see Him with their own eyes, and share in His miracles. It is not necessary to see the Lord with our human eyes in order to love Him, trust Him, and share His glory (1 Peter 1:8).

THIS FAITH IS IN A PERSON (1:1-2). That Person is Jesus Christ, the Son of God, the Saviour. From the very outset of his letter, Peter affirmed the deity of Jesus Christ. "God" and "Our Saviour" are not two different Persons; they describe one Person, Jesus Christ. Paul used a similar expression in Titus 2:10 and 3:4.

Peter reminded his readers that Jesus Christ is the Saviour by repeating this exalted title in 1:11, 2:20, 3:2, and 3:18. A *savior* is "one who brings salvation," and the word *salvation* was familiar to the people of that day. In their vocabulary, it meant "deliverance from trouble," particularly "deliverance from the enemy." It also carried the idea of "health and safety." A physician was looked on as a savior because he helped deliver the body from pain and limitations. A victorious general was a savior because he delivered the people from defeat. Even a wise official was a savior because he kept the nation in order and delivered it from confusion and decay.

It requires little insight to see how the title "Saviour" applies to our Lord Jesus Christ. He is, indeed, the Great Physician who heals the heart from the sickness of sin. He is the victorious conqueror who has defeated our enemies—sin, death, Satan, and hell—and is leading us in triumph (2 Cor. 2:14ff). He is "God and our Saviour" (2 Peter 1:1), "our Lord and Saviour" (1:11), and "the Lord and Saviour" (2:20). In order to be our Saviour, He had to give His life on the cross and die for the sins of the world.

Our Lord Jesus Christ has three "spiritual commodities" that can be secured from nobody else: righteousness, grace, and peace. When you trust Him as your Saviour, His righteousness becomes your righteousness and you are given a right standing before God (2 Cor. 5:21). You could never *earn* this righteousness; it is the gift of God to those who believe. "Not by works of righteousness which we have done, but according to His mercy He saved us" (Titus 3:5).

Grace is God's favor to the undeserving. God in His mercy does not give us what we do deserve; God in His grace gives us what we don't deserve. Our God is "the God of all grace" (1 Peter 5:10), and He channels that grace to us through Jesus Christ (John 1:16).

The result of this experience is *peace*, peace *with* God (Rom. 5:1) and the peace *of* God (Phil. 4:6-7). In fact, God's grace and peace are "multiplied" toward us as we walk with Him and trust His promises.

THIS FAITH INVOLVES GOD'S POWER (1:3). The Christian life begins with saving faith, faith in the Person of Jesus Christ. But when you know Jesus Christ personally, you also experience God's power, and this power produces "life and godliness." The unsaved sinner is dead (Eph. 2:1-3) and only Christ can raise him from the dead (John 5:24). When Jesus raised Lazarus from the dead, He said, "Loose him, and let him go" (John 11:44). Get rid of the graveclothes!

When you are born into the family of God by faith in Christ, you are born complete. God gives you everything you will ever need "for life and godliness." Nothing has to be added! "And ye are complete in Him" (Col. 2:10). The false teachers claimed that they had a "special doctrine" that would add something to the lives of Peter's readers, but Peter knew that *nothing could be added.* Just as a normal baby is born with all the "equipment" he needs for life and only needs to grow, so the Christian has all that is needed and only needs to grow. God never has to call back any of His "models" because something is lacking or faulty.

Just as a baby has a definite genetic structure that determines how he will grow, so the believer is "genetically structured" to experience "glory and virtue." One day he will be like the Lord Jesus Christ (Rom. 8:29; 1 John 3:2). We have been "called . . . to His eternal glory" (1 Peter 5:10), and we shall share that glory when Jesus Christ returns and takes His people to heaven.

But we are also "called . . . to virtue." We have been saved so that we might "show forth the praises [virtues] of Him who hath called [us] out of darkness into His marvelous light" (1 Peter 2:9). We should not wait until we get to heaven to become like Jesus Christ! In our character and conduct, we should reveal His beauty and grace today.

THIS FAITH INVOLVES GOD'S PROMISES (1:4). God has not only given us all that we need for life and godliness, but He has also given us His Word to enable us to develop this life and godliness. These promises are *great* because they come from a great God and they lead to a great life. They are *precious* because their value is beyond calculation. If we lost the Word of God, there would be no way to replace it. Peter must have liked the word *precious,* for he wrote about the "precious faith" (2 Peter 1:1; cf. 1 Peter 1:7), the "precious promises" (2 Peter 1:4), the "precious blood" (1 Peter 1:19), the precious stone (1 Peter 2:4, 6), and the precious Saviour (1 Peter 2:7).

When the sinner believes on Jesus Christ, the Spirit of God uses the Word of God to impart the life and nature of God within. A baby shares the nature of its parents, and a person born of God shares the divine nature of God. The lost sinner is dead, but the Christian is alive because he shares the divine nature. The lost sinner is decaying because of his corrupt nature, but the Christian can experience a dynamic life of godliness because he has God's divine nature within. Mankind is under the bondage of corruption (Rom. 8:21), but the believer shares the freedom and growth that is a part of possessing the divine nature.

Nature determines *appetite*. The pig wants slop and the dog will even eat its own vomit (2 Peter 2:22), but the sheep desires green pastures. Nature also determines *behavior*. An eagle flies because it has an eagle's nature and a dolphin swims because that is the nature of the dolphin. Nature determines *environment:* squirrels climb trees, moles burrow underground, and trout swim in the water. Nature also determines *association:* lions travel in prides, sheep in flocks, and fish in schools.

If nature determines appetite, and we have God's nature within, then we ought to have an appetite for that which is pure and holy. Our behavior ought to be like that of the Father, and we ought to live in the kind of "spiritual environment" that is suited to our nature. We ought to associate with that which is true to our nature (see 2 Cor. 6:14ff). The only normal, fruit-bearing life for the child of God is a *godly* life.

Because we possess this divine nature, we have "completely escaped" the defilement and decay in this present evil world. If we feed the new nature the nourishment of the Word, then we will have little interest in the garbage of the world. But if we "make provision for the flesh" (Rom. 13:14), our sinful nature will lust after the "old sins" (2 Peter 1:9) and we will disobey God. Godly living is the result of cultivating the new nature within.

Faith Results in Spiritual Growth (2 Peter 1:5-7)

Where there is life, there must be growth. The new birth is not the end; it is the beginning. God gives His children all that they need to live godly lives, but His children must apply themselves and be diligent to use the "means of grace" He has provided. *Spiritual growth is not automatic.* It requires cooperation with God and the application of spiritual diligence and discipline. "Work out your own salvation. . . . For it is God which worketh in you" (Phil. 2:12-13).

Peter listed seven characteristics of the godly life, but we must not think of them as seven beads on a string or even seven stages of development. The word translated *add* really means "to supply generously." In other words, we develop one quality as we exercise another quality. These graces relate to each other the way the branch relates to the trunk and the twigs to the branch. Like the "fruit of the Spirit" (Gal. 5:22-23), these qualities grow out of life and out of a vital relationship with Jesus Christ. It is not enough for the Christian to "let go and let God," as though spiritual growth were God's work alone. Literally, Peter wrote, "Make every effort to bring alongside." The Father and the child must work together.

The first quality of character Peter listed was *virtue.* We met this word in verse 3, and it basically means "excellence." To the Greek philosophers, it meant "the fulfillment of a thing." When anything in nature fulfills its purpose, that is "virtue—moral excellence." The word was also used to describe the power of the gods to do heroic deeds. The land that produces crops is "excellent" because it is fulfilling its purpose. The tool that works correctly is "excellent" because it is doing what a tool is supposed to do.

A Christian is supposed to glorify God because he has God's nature within; so, when he does this, he shows "excellence" because he is fulfilling his purpose in life. True virtue in the Christian life is not "polishing" human qualities, no matter how fine they may be, but producing *divine* qualities that make the person more like Jesus Christ.

Faith helps us develop virtue, and virtue helps us develop *knowledge* (2 Peter 1:5). The word translated *knowledge* in verses 2 and 3 means "full knowledge" or "knowledge that is growing." The word used here suggests *practical* knowledge or discernment. It refers to the ability to handle life success-fully. It is the opposite of being "so heavenly minded as to be of no earthly good!" This kind of knowledge does not come automatically. It comes from obedience to the will of God (John 7:17). In the Christian life, you must not separate the heart and the mind, character and knowledge.

Temperance is the next quality on Peter's list of spiritual virtues, and it means self-control. "He that is slow to anger is better than the mighty; and he that ruleth his spirit than he that taketh a city" (Prov. 16:32). "He that hath no rule over his own spirit is like a city that is broken down and without walls" (Prov. 25:28). Paul in his letters often com-pared the Christian to an athlete who must exercise and discipline himself if he ever hopes to win the prize (1 Cor. 9:24-27; Phil. 3:12-16; 1 Tim. 4:7-8).

Patience is the ability to endure when circumstances are difficult. Self-control has to do with handling the *pleasures* of life, while patience relates primarily to the *pressures* and *problems* of life. (The ability to endure problem people is "long-suffering.") Often, the person who "gives in" to plea-sures is not disciplined enough to handle pressures either, so he "gives up."

Patience is not something that develops automatically; we must work at it. James 1:2-8 gives us the right approach. We must expect trials to come, because without trials we could never learn patience. We must, by faith, let our trials work *for* us and not against us, because we know that God is at work in our trials. If we need wisdom in making decisions, God will grant that wisdom if we ask Him. Nobody enjoys trials, but we do enjoy the confidence we can have in trials that God is at work, causing everything to work together for our good and His glory.

Godliness simply means "God-likeness." In the original Greek, this word meant "to worship well." It described the man who was right in his relationship with God and with his fellow man. Perhaps the words *reverence* and *piety* come closer to defining this term. It is that quality of character that makes a person distinctive. He lives above the petty things of life, the passions and pressures that control the lives of others. He seeks to do the will of God and, as he does, he seeks the welfare of others.

We must never get the idea that godliness is an impractical thing, because it is intensely practical. The godly person makes the kinds of decisions that are right and noble. He does not take an easy path simply to avoid either pain or trial. He does what is right because it is right and because it is the will of God.

Brotherly kindness (*philadelphia* in the Greek) is a virtue that Peter must have acquired the hard way, for the disciples of our Lord often debated and disagreed with one another. If we love Jesus Christ, we must also love the brethren. We should practice an "unfeigned [sincere] love of the brethren" (1 Peter 1:22) and not just pretend that we love them. "Let brotherly love continue" (Heb. 13:1). "Be kindly affectioned one to another with brotherly love" (Rom. 12:10). The fact that we love our brothers and sisters in Christ is one evidence that we have been born of God (1 John 5:1-2).

But there is more to Christian growth than brotherly love; we must also have the sacrificial love that our Lord displayed when He went to the cross. The kind of love ("charity") spoken of in verse 7 is agape love, the kind of love that God shows toward lost sinners. This is the love that is described in 1 Corinthians 13, the love that the Holy Spirit produces in our hearts as we walk in the Spirit (Rom. 5:5; Gal. 5:22). When we have *brotherly* love, we love because of our likenesses to others; but with *agape* love, we love in spite of the differences we have.

It is impossible for fallen human nature to manufacture these seven qualities of Christian character. They must be produced by the Spirit of God. To be sure, there are unsaved people who possess amazing self-control and endurance, but these virtues point to *them* and not to the Lord. *They* get the glory. When God produces the beautiful nature of His Son in a Christian, it is God who receives the praise and glory.

Because we have the divine nature, we can grow spiritually and develop this kind of Christian character. It is through the power of God and the precious promises of God that this growth takes place. The divine "genetic structure" is already there: God wants us to be "conformed to the image of His Son" (Rom. 8:29). The life within will reproduce that image if we but diligently cooperate with God and use the means He has lavishly given us.

And the amazing thing is this: as the image of Christ is reproduced in us, the process does not destroy our own personalities. We still remain uniquely ourselves!

One of the dangers in the church today is imitation. People have a tendency to become like their pastor, or like a church leader, or perhaps like some "famous Christian." As they do this, they destroy their own uniqueness while failing to become like Jesus Christ. They lose both ways! Just as each child in a family resembles his parents and yet is different, so each child in God's family comes more and more to resemble Jesus Christ and yet is different. Parents don't duplicate themselves, they reproduce themselves; and wise parents permit their children to be themselves.

Spiritual Growth Brings Practical Results
(2 Peter 1:8-11)

How can the believer be certain that he is growing spiritually? Peter gave three evidences of true spiritual growth.

FRUITFULNESS (1:8). Christian character is an end in itself, but it is also a means to an end. The more we become like Jesus Christ, the more the Spirit can use us in witness and service. The believer who is not growing is idle ("barren") and unfruitful. His knowledge of Jesus Christ is producing nothing practical in his life. The word translated *idle* also means "ineffective." The people who fail to grow usually fail in everything else!

Some of the most effective Christians I have known are people without dramatic talents and special abilities, or even exciting personalities; yet God has used them in a marvelous way. Why? Because they are becoming more and more like Jesus Christ. They have the kind of character and conduct that God can trust with blessing. They are fruitful because they are faithful; they are effective because they are growing in their Christian experience.

These beautiful qualities of character do exist "within us" because we possess the divine nature. We must cultivate them so that they increase and produce fruit in and through our lives.

VISION (1:9). Nutritionists tell us that diet can certainly affect vision and this is especially true in the spiritual realm. The unsaved person is in the dark because Satan has blinded his mind (2 Cor. 4:3-4). A person has to be born again before his eyes are opened and he can see the kingdom of God (John 3:3). But after our eyes are opened, it is important that we increase our vision and see all that God wants us to see. The phrase *cannot see afar off* is the translation of a word that means "shortsighted." It is the picture of some-body closing or squinting his eyes, unable to see at a distance.

There are some Christians who see only their own church, or their own denomination, but who fail to see the greatness of God's family around the world. Some believers see the needs at home but have no vision for a lost world. Someone asked Phillips Brooks what he would do to revive a dead church, and he replied, "I would preach a missionary ser-mon and take up a collection!" Jesus admonished His disci-ples, "Lift up your eyes, and look on the fields; for they are white already to harvest" (John 4:35).

Some congregations today are like the church at Laodicea: they are proud that they are "rich and increased with goods, and have need of nothing," and do not realize that they are "wretched, and miserable, and poor, and blind, and naked" (Rev. 3:17). It is a tragedy to be "spiritually nearsighted," but it is even a greater tragedy to be blind!

If we forget what God has done for us, we will not be excited to share Christ with others. Through the blood of Jesus Christ we have been purged and forgiven! God has opened our eyes! Let's not forget what He has done! Rather, let's cultivate gratitude in our hearts and sharpen our spiri-tual vision. Life is too brief and the needs of the world too great for God's people to be walking around with their eyes closed!

SECURITY (1:10-11). If you walk around with your eyes closed, you will stumble! But the growing Christian walks with confidence because he knows he is secure in Christ. It is not our profession of faith that guarantees that we are saved; it is our progression in the faith that gives us that assurance. The person who claims to be a child of God but whose character and conduct give no evidence of spiritual growth is deceiving himself and heading for judgment.

Peter pointed out that "calling" and "election" go together. The same God who *elects* His people also ordains the means to *call* them. The two must go together, as Paul wrote to the Thessalonians: "God hath from the beginning chosen you to salvation. . . . Whereunto He called you by our Gospel" (2 Thes. 2:13-14). We do not preach election to unsaved people; we preach the Gospel. But God uses that Gospel to call sinners to repentance, and then those sinners discover that they were chosen by God!

Peter also pointed out that election is no excuse for spiritual immaturity or for lack of effort in the Christian life. Some believers say, "What is going to be is going to be. There is nothing we can do." But Peter admonishes us to "be diligent." This means "make every effort." (He used this same verb in 2 Peter 1:5.) While it is true that God must work in us before we can do His will (Phil. 2:12-13), it is also true that we must *be willing* for God to work, and we must cooperate with Him. Divine election must never be an excuse for human laziness.

The Christian who is sure of his election and calling will never "stumble" but will prove by a consistent life that he is truly a child of God. He will not always be on the mountaintop, but he will always be climbing higher. If we do "these things" (the things listed in 2 Peter 1:5-7, cf. v. 8), if we display Christian growth and character in our daily lives, then we can be sure we are converted and will one day be in heaven.

In fact, the growing Christian can look forward to "an abundant entrance" into the eternal kingdom! The Greeks used this phrase to describe the welcome given Olympic winners when they returned home. Every believer will arrive in heaven, but some will have a more glorious welcome than others. Alas, some believers "shall be saved, yet so as by fire" (1 Cor. 3:15).

The word *ministered* in 2 Peter 1:11 is the same as the word *add* in verse 5, and is the translation of a Greek word that means "to bear the expenses of a chorus." When the Greek theatrical groups presented their dramas, somebody had to underwrite the expenses, which were very great. The word came to mean "to make lavish provision." If we make lavish provision to grow spiritually (v. 5), then God will make lavish provision for us when we enter heaven!

Just think of the blessings that the growing Christian enjoys: fruitfulness, vision, security—and heaven's best! All this and heaven too!

The Christian life begins with faith, but that faith must lead to spiritual growth—unless it is dead faith. But dead faith is not saving faith (James 2:14-26). Faith leads to growth and growth leads to practical results in life and service. People who have this kind of Christian experience are not likely to fall prey to apostate false teachers.

2

Wake Up
and Remember!

2 Peter 1:12-21

The best defense against false teaching is true living. A church filled with growing Christians, vibrant in their faith, is not likely to fall prey to apostates with their counterfeit Christianity. But this Christian living must be based on the authoritative Word of God. False teachers find it easy to seduce people who do not know their Bible but who are desirous of "experiences" with the Lord. It is a dangerous thing to build on subjective experience alone and ignore objective revelation.

Peter discussed Christian experience in the first half of 2 Peter 1, and in the last half he discussed the revelation we have in the Word of God. His purpose is to show the importance of knowing God's Word and relying on it completely. The Christian who knows what he believes and why he believes it will rarely be seduced by the false teachers and their devious doctrines.

Peter underscores the dependability and durability of the Word of God by contrasting Scripture with men, experiences, and the world.

Men Die, but the Word Lives (2 Peter 1:12-15)

Through their preaching and teaching, the apostles and New Testament prophets laid the foundation of the church (Eph. 2:20) and we in later generations are building on that foundation. However, the men were not the foundation; Jesus Christ is the foundation (1 Cor. 3:11). He is also the chief cornerstone that ties the building together (Eph. 2:20). If the church is to last, it cannot be built on mere men. It must be built on the Son of God.

Our Lord had told Peter when he would die and how he would die. "When thou shalt be old, thou shalt stretch forth thy hands, and another shall gird thee, and carry thee whither thou wouldest not" (John 21:18). This explains why, shortly after Pentecost, Peter was able to sleep in prison the night before he was scheduled to be killed; he knew that Herod could not take his life (Acts 12:1ff). Tradition says that Peter was crucified in Rome. Like all of God's faithful servants, Peter was immortal until his work was done.

There were at least three motives behind Peter's ministry as he wrote this letter. The first was *obedience to Christ's command.* "I will not be negligent" (2 Peter 1:12). "When thou art converted," Jesus had said to Peter, "Strengthen thy brethren" (Luke 22:32). Peter knew that he had a special ministry to fulfill.

His second motive was simply that this reminder was *the right thing to do.* "I think it meet," he wrote, which simply means, "I think it is right and suitable." It is always right to stir up the saints and remind them of the Word of God!

His third motive is wrapped up in the word *endeavor* in 2 Peter 1:15. It is the same word that is translated *diligence* in verses 5 and 10. It means "to hasten to do something, to be zealous in doing it." Peter knew that he would soon die, so he wanted to take care of his spiritual responsibilities before it was too late. You and I do not know when we will die, so we had better start being diligent today!

What was it that Peter wanted to accomplish? The answer is found in the word that is repeated in verses 12, 13, and 15—*remembrance*. Peter wanted to impress his readers' minds with the Word of God so that they would never forget it! "I think it meet . . . to stir you up by putting you in remembrance" (1:13). The verb *stir you up* means "to awaken, to arouse." This same word is used to describe a storm on the Sea of Galilee! (John 6:18) Peter knew that our minds have a tendency to get accustomed to truth and then to take it for granted. We forget what we ought to remember, and we remember what we ought to forget!

The readers of this letter knew the truth and were even "established" in it (2 Peter 1:12), but that was no guarantee they would always remember the truth and apply it. One reason the Holy Spirit was given to the church was to remind believers of the lessons already learned (John 14:26). In my own radio ministry, I have received letters from listeners who get upset when I repeat something. In my reply, I often refer them to what Paul wrote in Philippians 3:1—"To write the same things to you, to me indeed is not grievous, but for you it is safe." Our Lord often repeated Himself as He taught the people, and He was a Master Teacher.

Peter knew that he was going to die, so he wanted to leave behind something that would never die—the written Word of God. His two epistles became a part of the inspired Scriptures, and they have been ministering to the saints for centuries. Men die, but the Word of God lives on!

It is possible that Peter was also alluding to the Gospel of Mark. Most Bible scholars believe that the Spirit used Peter to give John Mark some of the data for his book (see 1 Peter 5:13). One of the church fathers, Papias, said that Mark was "Peter's disciple and interpreter."

The church of Jesus Christ is always one generation away

from extinction. If there were no dependable written revelation, we would have to depend on word-of-mouth tradition. If you have ever played the party game "Gossip," you know how a simple sentence can be radically changed when passed from one person to another! We do not depend on the traditions of dead men; we depend on the truth of the living Word. Men die, but the Word lives forever.

If we did not have a dependable written revelation, the church would be at the mercy of men's memories. People who pride themselves on having good memories should sit on the witness stand in a courtroom! It is amazing that three perfectly honest witnesses can, with good conscience, give three different accounts of an automobile accident! Our memories are defective and selective. We usually remember what we want to remember, and often we distort even that.

Fortunately, we can depend on the written Word of God. "It is written" and it stands written forever. We can be saved through this living Word (1 Peter 1:23-25), nurtured by it (1 Peter 2:2), and guided and protected as we trust and obey.

Experiences Fade, but the Word Remains
(2 Peter 1:16-18)

The focus in this paragraph is on the transfiguration of Jesus Christ. The experience is recorded by Matthew (17:1ff), Mark (9:2-8), and Luke (9:28-36); yet none of those writers actually participated in it! Peter was there when it happened! In fact, the very words that he used in this section (2 Peter 1:12-18) remind us of his experience on the Mount of Transfiguration. He used the word *tabernacle* twice (vv. 13-14), and this suggests Peter's words, "Let us make here three tabernacles" (Matt. 17:4). In 2 Peter 1:15, he used the word *decease*, which is "exodus" in the Greek and is used in Luke 9:31. Jesus did not consider His death on the cross a defeat;

rather, it was an "exodus"—He would deliver His people from bondage the way Moses delivered Israel from Egypt! Peter wrote of his own death as an "exodus," a release from bondage.

Note the repetition of the pronoun *we* in 2 Peter 1:16-19. It refers to Peter, James, and John—the only apostles with the Lord on the Mount of Transfiguration. (John referred to this experience in John 1:14—"We beheld His glory.") These three men had to keep silent about their experience until after the Lord was raised from the dead (Matt. 17:9); then they told the other believers what had happened on the mountain.

What was the significance of the Transfiguration? For one thing, it confirmed Peter's testimony about Jesus Christ (Matt. 16:13-16). Peter saw the Son in His glory, and he heard the Father speak from heaven, "This is My beloved Son, in whom I am well pleased" (2 Peter 1:17). First we put our faith in Christ and confess Him, and then He gives us wonderful confirmation.

The Transfiguration also had a special significance for Jesus Christ, who was nearing Calvary. It was the Father's way of strengthening His Son for that terrible ordeal of being the sacrifice for the sins of the world. The Law and the Prophets (Moses and Elijah) pointed to His ministry, and now He would fulfill those Scriptures. The Father spoke from heaven and assured the Son of His love and approval. The Transfiguration was proof that suffering leads to glory when we are in the will of God.

But there is a third message, and it has to do with the promised kingdom. In all three Gospels where the account of the Transfiguration is recorded, it is introduced with a statement about the kingdom of God (Matt. 16:28; Mark 9:1; Luke 9:27). Jesus promised that, before they died, some of the disciples would see the kingdom of God in power! This took place on the Mount of Transfiguration when our Lord revealed His glory. It was a word of assurance to the disciples, who could not understand our Lord's teaching about the Cross. If He were to die, what would happen to the promised kingdom that He had been preaching about all those months?

Now we can understand why Peter used this event in his letter: he was refuting the false teachings of the apostates that the kingdom of God would never come (2 Peter 3:3ff). These false teachers denied the promise of Christ's coming! In the place of God's promises, these counterfeits put "cunningly devised fables" (1:16) that robbed the believers of their blessed hope.

The word *fables* means "myths," manufactured stories that have no basis in fact. The Greek and Roman world abounded in stories about the gods, mere human speculations that tried to explain the world and its origin. No matter how interesting these myths might be, the Christian is not to heed them (1 Tim. 1:4), but refuse them (1 Tim. 4:7). Paul warned Timothy that the time would come in the church when professed Christians would not want to hear true doctrine, but would "turn away their ears from the truth, and . . . be turned unto fables [myths]" (2 Tim. 4:4). Paul also warned Titus about "Jewish fables [myths]" (Titus 1:14), so even some of the Jews had abandoned their sacred Scriptures and accepted man-made substitutes.

Peter wrote a summary of what he saw and heard on the Mount of Transfiguration. He saw Jesus Christ robed in majestic glory, and therefore witnessed a demonstration of the "power and coming" of the Lord Jesus Christ. When Jesus Christ came to earth at Bethlehem, He did not display His glory openly. To be sure, He revealed His glory in His miracles (John 2:11), but even this was primarily for the sake of His disciples. His face did not shine, nor did He have a halo over His head. "He hath no form nor comeliness; and when we shall see Him, there is no beauty that we should desire Him" (Isa. 53:2).

Peter not only saw Christ's glory, but he heard the Father's voice "from the magnificent glory." Witnesses are people who tell accurately what they have seen and heard (Acts 4:20), and Peter was a faithful witness. Is Jesus Christ of Nazareth the Son of God? Yes, He is! How do we know? The Father said so!

You and I were not eyewitnesses of the Transfiguration. Peter was there, and he faithfully recorded his experience for us in the letter that he wrote, inspired by the Spirit of God. Experiences fade, but the Word of God remains! Experiences are subjective, but the Word of God is objective. Experiences may be interpreted in different ways by different participants, but the Word of God gives one clear message. What we remember about our experiences can be unconsciously distorted, but the Word of God remains the same and abides forever.

When we study 2 Peter 2, we will discover that apostate teachers try to turn people away from the Word of God and into "deeper experiences" that are contrary to the Word. These false teachers use "feigned words" instead of God's inspired Word (2:3), and they teach "damnable heresies" (2:1). In other words, this is really a matter of life and death! If a person believes the truth, he will live; if he believes lies, he will die. It is the difference between salvation and condemnation.

By reminding his readers of the Transfiguration, Peter affirmed several important doctrines of the Christian faith. He affirmed that Jesus Christ is indeed the Son of God. The test of any religion is, "What do you say about Jesus Christ?" If a religious teacher denies the deity of Christ, then he is a false teacher (1 John 2:18-29; 4:1-6).

But the Person of Jesus Christ is only one test; we must

also ask, "And what is the work of Jesus Christ? Why did He come and what did He do?" Again, the Transfiguration gives us the answer; for Moses and Elijah "appeared in glory, and spake of His decease [exodus] which He should accomplish at Jerusalem" (Luke 9:31). His death was not simply an example, as some liberal theologians want us to believe; it was an exodus, an accomplishment. He accomplished something on the cross—the redemption of lost sinners!

The Transfiguration was also affirmation of the truth of the Scriptures. Moses represented the Law; Elijah represented the Prophets; both pointed to Jesus Christ (Heb. 1:1-3). He fulfilled the Law and the Prophets (Luke 24:27). We believe the Bible because Jesus believed the Bible and said it was the Word of God. Those who question the truth and authority of the Scriptures are not arguing with Moses, Elijah, or Peter, but with the Lord Jesus Christ.

This event also affirmed the reality of God's kingdom. We who have a completed Bible can look back and understand the progressive lessons that Jesus gave His disciples about the Cross and the kingdom, but at that time those twelve men were very confused. They did not understand the relationship between His suffering and His glory (Peter's first epistle discusses this theme) and the church and the kingdom. At the Transfiguration, our Lord made it clear to His followers that His suffering *would lead to glory* and that the cross would ultimately result in the crown.

There was also a very practical lesson that Peter, James, and John needed to learn, because each of these would also suffer. James was the first of the apostles to die (Acts 12:1-2). John lived a long life but it led to exile and suffering (Rev. 1:9). Peter suffered for the Lord during his ministry, and then laid down his life just as the Lord had prophesied. On the Mount of Transfiguration, Peter, James, and John learned that suffering and glory go together, and that the Father's special love and approval are given to those who are willing to suffer for the sake of the Lord. We need this same lesson today.

Peter could not share his experience with us, but he could share the record of that experience so that we could have it permanently in the Word of God. It is not necessary for us to try to duplicate these experiences; in fact, such attempts would be dangerous, for the devil could give us a counterfeit experience that could lead us astray.

Remember Peter's wonderful news at the beginning of this letter: "like precious faith." This means that our faith gives us "an equal standing" with the apostles! They did not travel first-class and leave us to travel second-class! "Like precious faith *with us*" is what he wrote (italics mine). We were not on the Mount of Transfiguration, but we can still benefit from that experience as we meditate on it and permit the Spirit of God to reveal the glories of Jesus Christ.

We have learned two important truths as we have seen these contrasts: men die, but the Word lives, and experiences fade, but the Word remains. Peter added a third contrast.

The World Darkens, but the Word Shines
(2 Peter 1:19-21)

In some respects, the world is getting better. I thank God for the advances in medicine, transportation, and communication. I can speak to more people in one radio program than the apostles preached to in their entire lifetimes. I can write books that can be spread abroad and even translated into different languages. In areas of scientific achievement, the world has made great progress. But the human heart is still wicked, and all of our improvements in means have not improved our lives. Medical science enables people to live longer, but there is no guarantee they will live better. Modern means of communication only enable lies to travel faster! And jet planes enable us to get places faster, but we do not have better places to go!

We should not be surprised that our world is engulfed in spiritual darkness. In the Sermon on the Mount our Lord warned that there would be counterfeits who would invade the church with their false doctrines (Matt. 7:13-29). Paul gave a similar warning to the elders of Ephesus (Acts 20:28-35), and he gave further warnings when he wrote his epistles (Rom. 16:17-20; 2 Cor. 11:1-15; Gal. 1:1-9; Phil. 3:17-21; Col. 2; 1 Tim. 4; 2 Tim. 3—4. Even John, the great "apostle of love," warned about antichristian teachers who would seek to destroy the church (1 John 2:18-29; 4:1-6).

In other words, the apostles did not expect the world to get better and better either morally or spiritually. They all warned the church that false teachers would invade the local churches, introduce false doctrines, and lead many people astray. The world would get darker and darker; but as it did, the Word of God would shine brighter and brighter.

Peter made three affirmations about this Word.

IT IS THE SURE WORD (1:19a). Peter was not suggesting that the Bible is more certain than the experience he had on the Mount of Transfiguration. His experience was real and true, and the record in the Bible is dependable. As we have seen, the Transfiguration was a demonstration of the promise given in the prophetic Word; and this promise now has added certainty because of what Peter experienced. The Transfiguration experience corroborated the prophetic promises. The apostates would attempt to discredit the promise of His coming (3:3ff), but the Scriptures were sure. For, after all, the promise of the kingdom was reaffirmed by Moses, Elijah, the Son of God, and the Father! And the Holy Spirit wrote the record for the church to read!

"The testimony of the Lord is sure" (Ps. 19:7). "Thy testimonies are very sure" (Ps. 93:5). "All His commandments are sure" (Ps. 111:7). "Therefore I esteem all Thy precepts concerning all things to be right; and I hate every false way" (Ps. 119:128).

It is interesting to put together 2 Peter 1:16 and 19: "For we have not followed cunningly devised fables. . . . We have also a more sure word of prophecy." As I travel, I often meet zealous cultists in airports, all of whom want me to buy their books. I always refuse because I have the sure Word of God and have no need for the religious fables of men. " 'What is the chaff to the wheat?' saith the Lord" (Jer. 23:28).

But one day I found one of those books, left behind in the men's room, so I decided to take it with me and read it. How anybody could believe such foolish fables is more than I can understand. The book claimed to be based on the Bible, but the writer so twisted the Scriptures that the verses quoted ended up meaning only what he wanted them to mean. Cunningly devised fables! Yet there was spiritual death between those covers to anyone who would believe those lies.

IT IS THE SHINING WORD (1:19b). Peter called the world "a dark place," and the word he used means "murky." It is the picture of a dank cellar or a dismal swamp. Human history began in a lovely garden, but that garden today is a murky swamp. What you see when you look at this world system is an indication of the spiritual condition of your heart. We still see beauty in God's creation, but we see no beauty in what mankind is doing with God's creation. Peter did not see this world as a Garden of Eden, nor should we.

God is light and His Word is light. "Thy word is a lamp unto my feet, and a light unto my path" (Ps. 119:105). When Jesus Christ began His ministry, "the people which sat in darkness saw great light" (Matt. 4:16). His coming into this world was the dawning of a new day (Luke 1:78). We Christians are the light of the world (Matt. 5:14-16), and it is our privilege and responsibility to hold forth the Word of life— God's light—so that men might see the way and be saved (Phil. 2:14-16).

As believers, we must heed this Word and govern our lives by what it says. For unbelievers, things will get darker and darker, until they end up in eternal darkness; but God's people are looking for the return of Jesus Christ and the dawning of the new day of glory. The false teachers scoffed at the idea of Christ's return and the dawning of a new day, but Peter affirmed the truth of the sure Word of God. "But the Day of the Lord will come as a thief in the night" (2 Peter 3:10).

Before the day dawns, the "day star" (or morning star) shines brightly as the herald of the dawn. To the church, Jesus Christ is "the bright and morning star" (Rev. 22:16). The promise of His coming shines brightly, no matter how dark the day may be (see Num. 24:17). He is also the "sun of righteousness," who will bring healing to believers but judgment to unbelievers (Mal. 4:1-2). How thankful we ought to be for God's sure and shining Word, and how we ought to heed it in these dark days!

IT IS THE SPIRIT-GIVEN WORD (1:20-21). This is one of two important Scriptures affirming the divine inspiration of the Word of God. The other is 2 Timothy 3:14-17. Peter affirmed that the Scriptures were not written by men who used their own ideas and words, but by men of God who were "moved by the Holy Spirit." The word translated *moved* means "to be carried along, as a ship is carried by the wind." The Scriptures are "God-breathed"; they are not the inventions of men.

Again, Peter was refuting the doctrines of the apostates. They taught with "feigned words" (2 Peter 2:3) and twisted the Scriptures to make them mean something else (3:16).

They denied the promise of Christ's coming (3:3-4), and thus denied the very prophetic Scriptures.

Since the Spirit gave the Word, only the Spirit can teach the Word and interpret it accurately (see 1 Cor. 2:14-15). Of course, every false teacher claims that he is "led by the Spirit," but his handling of the Word of God soon exposes him. Since the Bible did not come by the will of man, it cannot be understood by the will of man. Even religious Nicodemus, a leading teacher among the Jews, was ignorant of the most essential doctrines of the Word of God (John 3:10-12).

In 2 Peter 1:20, Peter was not prohibiting the private study of the Bible. Some religious groups have taught that only the "spiritual leaders" may interpret Scripture, and they have used this verse as their defense. But Peter was not writing primarily about the interpretation of Scripture, but the origin of Scripture: it came by the Holy Spirit through holy men of God. And since it came by the Spirit, it must be taught by the Spirit.

The word translated *private* simply means "one's own" or "its own." The suggestion is, since all Scripture is inspired by the Spirit it must all "hang together" and no one Scripture should be divorced from the others. You can use the Bible to prove almost anything if you isolate verses from their proper context, which is exactly the approach the false teachers use. Peter stated that the witness of the apostles confirmed the witness of the prophetic Word; there is one message with no contradiction. Therefore, the only way these false teachers can "prove" their heretical doctrines is by misusing the Word of God. Isolated texts, apart from contexts, become pretexts.

The Word of God was written to common people, not to theological professors. The writers assumed that common people could read it, understand it, and apply it, led by the same Holy Spirit who inspired it. The humble individual believer can learn about God as he reads and meditates on the Word of God; he does not need the "experts" to show him truth. However, this does not deny the ministry of teachers in the church (Eph. 4:11), special people who have a gift for explaining and applying the Scriptures. Nor does it deny the "collective wisdom" of the church as, over the ages, these doctrines have been defined and refined. Teachers and creeds have their place, but they must not usurp the authority of the Word over the conscience of the individual believer.

Until the day dawns, we must be sure that the love for His coming is like a shining star in our hearts (2 Peter 1:19). Unless we love His appearing, we will not look for His appearing; and it is the Word that keeps that expectation bright.

Men die, but the Word lives. Experiences fade, but the Word remains. The world grows darker, but the prophetic light shines brighter. The believer who builds his life on the Word of God and who looks for the coming of the Saviour is not likely to be led astray by false teachers. He will be taught by the Spirit and grounded on the sure Word of God.

Peter's message is, "Wake up—and remember!" A sleeping church is the devil's playground. It is while men slept that the enemy came in and sowed the tares (Matt. 13:24ff). Peter went to sleep on the Mount of Transfiguration and almost missed the whole thing!

"Be alert!" is the apostle's message. "Wake up and remember!"

3

Beware of Counterfeits

2 Peter 2:1-9

One of the most successful rackets in the world today is that of selling "fake art." Even some of the finest galleries and private collections have been invaded by paintings that are clever counterfeits of the great masters. Publishers have also had their share of hoaxes, purchasing "genuine" manuscripts that weren't so genuine after all.

But counterfeits are nothing new. Satan is the "great imitator" (2 Cor. 11:13-15), and he has been hard at work ever since he deceived Eve in the Garden (Gen. 3:1-7; 2 Cor. 11:1-4). He has false Christians (Matt. 13:38; John 8:44), a false Gospel (Gal. 1:6-9), and even a false righteousness (Rom. 9:30–10:4). One day, he will present to the world a false Christ (2 Thes. 2).

The nation Israel was constantly being led astray by false prophets. Elijah had to contend with the prophets of Baal, but they promoted a pagan religion. It was the *Jewish* false prophets who did the most damage, for they claimed to speak for Jehovah God. Both Jeremiah and Ezekiel exposed this counterfeit ministry, but the people followed the pseudo-prophets just the same. Why? Because the religion of the false prophets was easy, comfortable, and popular. The fact that the false prophets preached a false peace did not worry the people (Jer. 6:14). That was the message they wanted to hear!

The apostles and prophets laid the foundation for the church and then passed from the scene (Eph. 2:20). This is why Peter wrote about false *teachers*, rather than false prophets, because there are still teachers in the church. It is not likely that church members would listen to a "prophet," but they would listen to a teacher of the Word. Satan always uses the approach that will succeed.

In order to warn us to be alert, Peter presented three aspects of this subject of false teachers in the church.

The False Teachers Described (2 Peter 2:1-3)

This is not a very pretty picture! When you read the Epistle of Jude, you will find him using similar language, and vivid language it is. Peter knew that the truth of God's Word and the false doctrines of the heretics simply could not coexist. There could be no compromise on his part, any more than a surgeon could compromise with a cancerous tumor in a patient's body.

DECEPTION (2:1a). This theme runs throughout the entire chapter. To begin with, these teachers' message is false; Peter called what they taught "destructive heresies." The word *heresy* originally meant simply "to make a choice," but then it came to mean "a sect, a party." Promoting a party spirit in a church is one of the works of the flesh (Gal. 5:20). Whenever a church member says to another member, "Are you on my side or the pastor's side?" he is promoting a party spirit and causing division. A false teacher forces you to make a choice between his doctrines and the doctrines of the true Christian faith.

Not only was their message false, but their methods were false. Instead of openly declaring what they believed, they came into the church under false colors and gave the impression that they were true to the Christian faith. "They secretly bring in alongside" is the literal translation. They do not throw out the truth immediately; they simply lay their false teachings alongside the truth and give the impression that they believe the fundamentals of the faith. Before long, they remove the true doctrine and leave their false doctrine in its place.

In 2 Peter 2:3, Peter pointed out that the false teachers used "feigned words." The Greek word is *plastos*, from which we get our English word *plastic*. Plastic words! Words that can be twisted to mean anything you want them to mean! The false teachers use our vocabulary, but they do not use our dictionary. They talk about "salvation," "inspiration," and the great words of the Christian faith, but they do not mean what we mean. Immature and untaught believers hear these preachers or read their books and think that these men are sound in the faith, but they are not.

Satan is a liar and his ministers are liars. They use the Bible, not to enlighten, but to deceive. They follow the same pattern Satan followed when he deceived Eve (Gen. 3:1-6). First, he questioned God's Word—"Yea, hath God said?" Then he denied God's Word—"Ye shall not surely die." Finally, he substituted his own lie—"Ye shall be as gods."

Keep in mind that these apostate teachers are not innocently ignorant of the Word, as was Apollos (Acts 18:24-28). They know the truth but they deliberately reject it. I read about a liberal pastor who was asked to read a paper at a ministerial conference on "Paul's views of justification." He read a paper that superbly presented the truth of the Gospel and justification by faith.

"I didn't know you believed that," a friend said to him

after the meeting.

"I don't believe it," the liberal pastor replied. "They didn't ask me for *my* views of justification. They asked for Paul's!"

DENIAL (2:1b). False teachers are better known for what they deny than what they affirm. They deny the inspiration of the Bible, the sinfulness of man, the sacrificial death of Jesus Christ on the cross, salvation by faith alone, and even the reality of eternal judgment. They especially deny the deity of Jesus Christ, for they know that if they can do away with His deity they can destroy the entire body of Christian truth. Christianity is Christ, and if He is not what He claims to be, there is no Christian faith.

It must be made clear that these false teachers are unsaved. They are compared to dogs and pigs, not to sheep (2:22). Jude describes these same people, and in verse 19 he clearly states, "having not the Spirit." If a person does not have the Spirit of God within, he is not a child of God (Rom. 8:9). He may pretend to be saved and even become a member or an officer in a fundamental church, but eventually he will deny the Lord.

In what sense were these people "bought" by the Lord? While it is true that Jesus Christ died for the church (Eph. 5:25), it is also true that He died for the sins of the whole world (1 John 2:2). He is the merchant who purchased the whole field (the world) that He might acquire the treasure in it (Matt. 13:44). When it comes to *application*, our Lord's atonement is limited to those who believe. But when it comes to *efficacy*, His death is sufficient for the whole world. He purchased even those who reject Him and deny Him! This makes their condemnation even greater.

Even good and godly Christians may disagree on fine points of doctrine, but they all agree on the person and work of Jesus Christ. He is the Son of God and God the Son. He is the only Saviour. To deny this is to condemn your own soul.

SENSUALITY (2:2). *Pernicious ways* simply means "licentious conduct." Jude accused the false teachers of "turning the grace of God into lasciviousness" (v. 4). Now we understand why they deny the truths of the Christian faith: they want to satisfy their own lusts and do it under the guise of religion. The false prophets in Jeremiah's day were guilty of the same sins (Jer. 23:14, 32).

The fact that *many* follow the evil example of their conduct is proof that people would rather follow the false than the true, the sensual rather than the spiritual. These false teachers are very successful in their ministry! They have glowing statistics to report and crowds gather to hear them! But statistics are not proof of authenticity. The broad way that leads to destruction is crowded (Matt. 7:13-14). Many will claim to be true servants of Christ, but will be rejected on the last day (Matt. 7:21-23).

What happens to their followers? For one thing, they bring disgrace to the name of Christ. The Christian faith gets a bad name because of their filthy lives. "They profess that they know God; but in works they deny Him, being abominable, and disobedient, and unto every good work reprobate" (Titus 1:16). "For the name of God is blasphemed among the Gentiles through you" (Rom. 2:24). Few things hinder the cause of Christ like the bad reputations of professing Christians who are members of orthodox churches.

GREED (2:3). False teachers are interested in one thing: making money. They exploit ("make merchandise of") ignorant people and use their religion as "a cloak of covetousness" (1 Thes. 2:5). Our Lord was a poor Man, and so were the apostles; yet they gave of themselves to minister to others. These false prophets are rich men who cleverly get others to minister to them! Micah described these false prophets in his day: "Her leaders pronounce judgment for a bribe, her priests instruct for a price, and her prophets divine for money" (Micah 3:11, NASB). Certainly the laborer is worthy of his hire (Luke 10:7), but his motives for ministry had better go beyond money. It has often been said that immorality, love of money, and pride have been the ruin of many people. These false teachers were guilty of all three!

They use their "plastic words" as well as "great swelling words" (2 Peter 2:18) to fascinate and influence their victims. They flatter sinners and tell them the kind of ego-building words that they want to hear (see the contrast in 1 Thes. 2:5). They will scratch the itching ears of people who reject the truth of the Bible and turn to fables (2 Tim. 4:1-4). Religion can be a tremendous tool for exploiting weak people, and these false teachers use religion just to get what they can. They are not ministers; they are merchandisers.

The true minister of Jesus Christ has nothing to hide: his life and ministry are an open book. He preaches the truth in love and does not twist the Scriptures to support his own selfish ideas. He does not flatter the rich or minister only to make money. Paul described the true minister in 2 Corinthians 4:2—"But [we] have renounced the hidden things of dishonesty, not walking in craftiness, nor handling the Word of God deceitfully; but by manifestation of the truth commending ourselves to every man's conscience in the sight of God." Contrast that description with what Peter wrote in this chapter, and with what Jude wrote, and you will see the difference. How we need to be alert and refuse to support ministries that exploit people and deny the Saviour.

The False Teachers Destroyed (2 Peter 2:3-6, 9)

Peter saw no hope for these apostates; their doom was sealed. His attitude was different from that of "tolerant" religious people today who say, "Well, they may not agree with us, but there are many roads to heaven." Peter made it clear that these false teachers had "forsaken the right way"

(2 Peter 2:15), which simply means they were going the *wrong* way! Their judgment was sure, even though it had not yet come. The trial was over, but the sentence had not yet been executed. It would not linger or slumber, Peter affirmed; it would come in due time.

In this section, Peter proved that judgment finally does come, no matter how secure the sinner might feel. He used three examples to verify this truth. (See also Jude 6-8.)

THE FALLEN ANGELS (2:4). We wish we knew more about the creation of the angels and the fall of Lucifer and his host, but most of these details are shrouded in mystery. Many Bible students believe that Isaiah 14:12-15 describes the fall of Lucifer, the highest of the angels. Some students feel that Ezekiel 28:11-19 also deals with the same topic. It would appear that Lucifer was God's deputy, in charge of the angelic hosts, but that his pride made him grasp after the very throne of God. (John Milton imaginatively portrayed this in the famous poem, *Paradise Lost.*) Revelation 12:4 suggests that perhaps one third of the angels fell with Lucifer, who became Satan, the adversary of God.

Where are these fallen angels now? We know that Satan is free and at work in the world (1 Peter 5:8), and that he has an army of demonic powers assisting him (Eph. 6:10-12), who are probably some of the fallen angels. But Peter said that some of the angels were confined to Tartarus ("hell"), which is a Greek word for the underworld. Tartarus may be a special section of hell where these angels are chained in pits of darkness, awaiting the final judgment. It is not necessary to debate the hidden mysteries of this verse in order to get the main message: God judges rebellion and will not spare those who reject His will. If God judged the angels, who in many respects are higher than men, then certainly He will judge rebellious men.

THE OLD WORLD (2:5). Genesis 6:3 indicates that God waited

120 years before He sent the flood. All during that time, Noah ministered as a "herald" of God's righteousness. If you want to read a description of the world before the flood, read Romans 1:18ff. Gentile civilization had become so corrupt that it was necessary for God to wipe the earth clean. He saved only eight people, Noah and his family, because they had faith in God (Heb. 11:7).

But nobody believed Noah's message! Jesus made it clear that people were enjoying their normal lives up to the very day that Noah and his family entered the ark! (Luke 17:26-27) No doubt there were plenty of "experts" who laughed at Noah and assured the people that a rainstorm was out of the question. Had anybody ever seen one? The apostates in Peter's day used that same argument to "prove" that the Day of the Lord would not come (2 Peter 3:3ff).

When you compare our world with Noah's world, you see some frightening parallels. The population was multiplying (Gen. 6:1), and the world was filled with wickedness (Gen. 6:5) and violence (Gen. 6:11, 13). Lawlessness abounded. True believers were a minority, and nobody paid any attention to them! But the flood came and the entire population of the world was destroyed. God does indeed judge those who reject His truth.

SODOM AND GOMORRAH (2:6). The record is given in Genesis 18—19, and God's opinion of the people of these cities is found in Genesis 13:13—"But the men of Sodom were wicked and sinners before the Lord exceedingly." Peter said they were "ungodly," and Jude said they were given to "fornication and going after strange flesh" (v. 7). The men of Sodom practiced filthy behavior and unlawful deeds (2 Peter 2:7-8). Since the Law of Moses had not yet been given, the word *unlawful* cannot refer to some Jewish law. In what sense were their filthy deeds "unlawful"? They were contrary to nature (see Rom. 1:24-27). The flagrant sin of Sodom and the other cities was unnatural sex, sodomy, or homosexual behavior, a sin that is clearly condemned in Scripture (Rom. 1:24-27; 1 Cor. 6:9; Lev. 18:22).

In spite of Abraham's intercessory prayer (Gen. 18:22ff) and Lot's last-minute warning, the people of Sodom perished in fire and brimstone. Again, up to the very minute that Lot left the city, the people were confident that everything was safe; but then the fire fell (Luke 17:28-29). God did not spare them, nor will He spare sinners today who willfully reject His truth and deny His Son. God buried Sodom and Gomorrah, probably under the Dead Sea. They are examples to sinners today to beware the wrath to come.

Having cited these three examples of certain judgment, Peter then applied the lesson to the subject at hand, *the false teachers* (2:9b). God has reserved the unjust for special punishment on that day of judgment. The false teachers may seem successful (for "many" follow them), but in the end, they will be condemned. Their judgment is being prepared now ("lingereth not," v. 3), and what is prepared will be reserved and applied on the last day.

What a contrast between the false teachers and the true children of God! We have an inheritance reserved for us (1 Peter 1:4) because Jesus Christ is preparing a home for us in heaven (John 14:1-6). We are not looking for judgment, but for the coming of the Lord to take His people home to glory! "For God hath not appointed us to wrath, but to obtain salvation by our Lord Jesus Christ" (1 Thes. 5:9).

Peter next turned his attention to the believers themselves. How could they stay true to the Lord in such a wicked world?

The True Believers Delivered (2 Peter 2:5-9)
Peter's purpose was not just to denounce the apostates; he also wanted to encourage the true believers. He once again

reached back into the Old Testament and cited two examples of deliverance.

NOAH (2:5). This man of faith experienced a twofold deliverance. First, God delivered him from the pollutions of the world around him. For 120 years, Noah faithfully proclaimed the Word of God to people who would not believe it. He and his family were surrounded by moral and spiritual darkness, yet they kept their lights shining. God did not protect Noah and his family by isolating them from the world, but by enabling them to remain pure in the midst of corruption. Through Jesus Christ, we too have "escaped the corruption that is in the world through lust" (1:4).

Our Lord petitioned the heavenly Father, "I pray not that Thou shouldest take them out of the world, but that Thou shouldest keep them from the evil" (John 17:15). Imagine Noah and his wife raising a family in a world so wicked that they could have no believing friends! Yet God found believing wives for their three sons, and God guarded this home from the pollutions of the world.

But God also delivered Noah and his family from the judgment of the world. The flood waters that brought condemnation to the world only lifted Noah and his household up above the judgment. They were secure in the ark of safety. In his first epistle, Peter had seen in the ark a type of our salvation in Jesus Christ (1 Peter 3:20-22). The world, as it were, was "buried" in the baptism of the flood, but Noah was lifted up, a picture of resurrection and salvation.

Certainly Peter was assuring his readers that, when the great day of judgment does come, they will be kept safe. Jesus Christ is our "ark of safety." He delivers us from the wrath to come (1 Thes. 1:10). God has promised that the earth will never again be judged by water, but there is coming a judgment of fire (2 Peter 3:10ff). But those who have trusted Christ will never face judgment (John 5:24), because

He bore their judgment on the cross.

LOT (2:6-8). Abraham took his nephew, Lot, with him when he left Ur and went to the land of Canaan, but Lot proved to be more of a problem than a blessing. When Abraham, in a lapse of faith, went down to Egypt, Lot went with him and got a taste of "the world" (Gen. 12:10—13:1). As Lot became richer, he had to separate from Abraham, and this removed him from his uncle's godly influence. What a privilege Lot had to walk with Abraham who walked with God! And yet, how Lot wasted his privileges.

When Lot had to choose a new area for his home, he measured it by what he had seen in Egypt (Gen. 13:10). Abraham took Lot out of Egypt, but he could not take Egypt out of Lot. Lot "pitched his tent toward Sodom" (Gen. 13:12), and then finally moved into Sodom (Gen. 14:12). God even used a local war to try to get Lot out of Sodom, but he went right back. That is where his heart was.

It is difficult for us to understand Lot. Peter made it clear that Lot was saved ("just Lot . . . that righteous man"), and yet we wonder what he was doing in such a wicked place as Sodom. If we understand Genesis 19 correctly, Lot had at least four daughters, two of whom had married men of Sodom. All the while Lot lived in Sodom, his soul was "tortured" and "greatly troubled" by the filthy conduct of the people. Perhaps he thought he could change them. If so, he failed miserably.

God enabled Lot and his family to remain unpolluted, even though they were living in the midst of a cesspool of iniquity. God also rescued Lot and two of his daughters before the judgment fell on Sodom and the other cities of the plain (Gen. 19). Lot was not rescued because of any merit on his part. He was rescued because he was a believer and because his Uncle Abraham had prayed for him. Abraham outside of Sodom had more influence than Lot inside the city. Lot even lost his testimony to his own family, for his married daughters and their husbands laughed at his warning, and his wife disobeyed God and was killed.

Lot *chose* to live in Sodom and could have avoided the filthy influence of the place, but many people today really have no choice and must live surrounded by the pollutions of the world. Think of the Christian slaves who had to serve godless masters, or Christian wives married to unsaved husbands, or believing children with unsaved parents. Christian employees working in offices or factories are forced to see and hear things that can easily stain the mind and heart. Peter assured his readers and us that God knows how to "be delivering the godly out of testing and temptation" (2 Peter 2:9, WUEST) so that we may live victoriously.

He also is able to rescue us from judgment. In Noah's case, it was a judgment of water, but in Lot's case it was a judgment of fire. The cities of the plain were caught in a violent overthrow as the area became a vast furnace of fire and brimstone. This certainly would parallel Peter's warning about the coming judgment of fire (3:10ff).

Peter was not pointing to Lot as an example of separated living, but rather as an example of one whom God rescued from pollution and condemnation. In a sense, Lot was even rescued against his will, because the angels had to grasp him by the hand and pull him out of the city (Gen. 19:16). Lot had entered Sodom, and then Sodom had entered Lot, and he found it difficult to leave.

Our Lord used both Noah and Lot to warn us to be prepared for His return (Luke 17:26-37). The people in Sodom were enjoying their regular pleasures, careless of the fact that judgment was coming; when it came, they were unprepared. "Wherefore, beloved, seeing that ye look for such things, be diligent that ye may be found of Him in peace, without spot, and blameless" (1 Peter 3:14).

But the same God who delivers the godly also reserves the ungodly for judgment. It has well been said that if God spares today's cities from judgment, He will have to apologize to Sodom and Gomorrah. Why is God's judgment lingering? Because God "is long-suffering . . . not willing that any should perish, but that all should come to repentance" (2 Peter 3:9). Society in Noah's day had 120 years in which to repent and believe, yet they rejected the truth. Though Lot's example and testimony were weak, he at least represented the truth; yet his immoral neighbors wanted nothing to do with God.

Our present age is not only like "the days of Noah," but it is also like "the days of Lot." Many believers have abandoned the place of separation and are compromising with the world. The professing church has but a weak testimony to the world and sinners do not really believe that judgment is coming. Society is full of immorality, especially the kind of sin for which Sodom was famous. It appears as though God is slumbering, unconcerned about the way rebellious sinners have polluted His world. But one day the fire will fall; then it will be too late.

God's people, as weak as they are, will be delivered from judgment by the grace and mercy of God. God could not judge Sodom until Lot and his family were out of the city. Likewise, it is my belief that God will not send wrath on this world until He takes His own people out and home to heaven. For God hath not appointed us to wrath, but to obtain salvation by our Lord Jesus Christ, who died for us, that, whether we wake or sleep [live or die], we should live together with Him" (1 Thes. 5:9-10)

One day soon, the fire will fall. Are you ready?

4

Marked Men

2 Peter 2:10-16

Peter is not yet finished with the apostates! Unlike some believers today, Peter was disturbed by the inroads the false teachers were making into the churches. He knew that their approach was subtle but their teachings were fatal, and he wanted to warn the churches about them.

Remember, however, that Peter opened this letter with positive teaching about salvation, Christian growth, and the dependability of the Word of God. He had a balanced ministry, and it is important that we maintain that balance today. When Charles Spurgeon started his magazine, he named it *The Sword and Trowel*, alluding to the workers in the Book of Nehemiah, who kept their swords in one hand and their tools in the other as they were repairing the walls of Jerusalem.

Some people have a purely negative ministry and never build anything. They are too busy fighting the enemy! Others claim to be "positive," but they never defend what they have built. Peter knew that it was not enough only to attack the apostates; he also had to give solid teaching to the believers in the churches.

In this section of his letter, Peter condemned the apostates for three specific sins.

Their Reviling (2 Peter 2:10-12)

The picture here is of proud people who try to build themselves up while they try to tear down everybody else. They show no respect for authority and are not afraid to attack and defame people in high positions.

God has established authority in this world, and when we resist authority, we are resisting God (Rom. 13:1ff). Parents are to have authority over their children (Eph. 6:1-4) and employers over their employees (Eph. 6:5-8). As citizens, we Christians should pray for those in authority (1 Tim. 2:1-4), show respect to them (1 Peter 2:11-17), and seek to glorify God in our behavior. As members of a local assembly, we should honor those who have the spiritual rule over us and seek to encourage them in their ministry (Heb. 13:7, 17; 1 Peter 5:1-6).

Human government is, in one sense, God's gift to help maintain order in the world, so that the church may minister the Word and win the lost to Christ (1 Tim. 2:1-8). We should pray daily for those in authority so that they might exercise that authority in the will of God. It is a serious thing for a Christian to oppose the law, and he must be sure he is in the will of God when he does it. He should also do it in a manner that glorifies Christ, so that innocent people (including unsaved government employees) might not be made to suffer.

THE REASON FOR THEIR REVILING (2:10). One word gives the reason: *flesh*. The depraved nature of man does not want to submit to any kind of authority. "Do your own thing!" is its insistent message, and many people follow it. In recent years, there has been an epidemic of books that encourage people to succeed at any cost, even to the extent of hurting or intimidating others. The important thing, according to these books, is to take care of yourself—"number one"—and to use other people as tools for the achievement of your own selfish goals.

Man's fallen nature encourages pride. When the ego is at stake, these apostates will stop at nothing in order to promote and protect themselves. Their attitude is completely opposite that of our Lord who willingly emptied Himself to become a servant, and then died as a sacrifice for our sins (see Phil. 2). These men that Peter described were *presumptuous*, which means they were "very daring and bold" in the way they spoke about those in positions of dignity. There is a boldness that is heroic, but there is also a boldness that is satanic.

These men were also *self-willed*, which means they "lived to please only themselves." They were arrogant and would even defy God to get what they wanted! Proverbs 21:24 describes them perfectly. While outwardly, they appeared to serve God and minister to the people, *inwardly* they fed their own egos and feathered their own nests.

In their arrogance, "they are not afraid to speak evil of dignities [glorious ones]." While the immediate reference is probably to "exalted ones" in places of authority, the angels may also be in view here, since in the next verse Peter referred to the angels. These apostates revile even the angels! And they do not even tremble when they do it! They are so secure in their pride, that they even dare God to judge them.

THE SERIOUSNESS OF THEIR REVILING (2:11). The angels are reviled by the apostates, but the apostates are not reviled by the angels! Even the angels, though greater in strength and power, will not intrude into a sphere that is not their own. The angels remember the rebellion of Lucifer and know how serious it is to revolt against God's authority. If God judged the rebellious angels, how much more will He judge rebellious men!

The suggestion here is that the godly angels do not even speak against the *fallen* angels. They have left all judgment to the Lord. We will learn more about this when we study Jude, for he mentions this matter of the angels in verses 8-9.

Speaking evil of others is a great sin, and the people of God must avoid it. We may not respect the people in office, but we must respect the office, for all authority is God-given. Those who revile government officials in the name of Christ ought to read and ponder Titus 3:1-2—"Remind them to be subject to rulers, to authorities, to be obedient, to be ready for every good deed, to malign no one, to be uncontentious, gentle, showing every consideration for all men" (NASB).

When Daniel refused the king's food, he did it in a gracious way that did not get his guard into trouble (Dan. 1). Even when the apostles refused to obey the Sanhedrin's order that they stop preaching in the name of Jesus, they acted like gentlemen. They respected the authority even though they disobeyed the order. It is when the flesh goes to work that pride enters in, and then we use our tongues as weapons instead of tools. "The words of his mouth are iniquity and deceit: he hath left off to be wise, and to do good" (Ps. 36:3).

THE JUDGMENT OF THEIR REVILING (2:12). Peter compared these false teachers to "unreasoning animals" (NASB) whose only destiny is to be slaughtered! At the end of this chapter, they are pictured as pigs and dogs! Animals have life, but they live purely by instinct. They lack the finer sensibilities that humans possess. Jesus warned us not to waste precious things on unappreciative brute beasts (Matt. 7:6).

I once made a pastoral visit at a home where a death had occurred, and even before I made it up the stairs to the door, a huge dog began to bark and carry on as though I were there to rob everybody. I ignored his threats because I knew he was acting purely on instinct. He was making a lot of noise about something he knew nothing about! His master had to take him to the basement before it was safe for me to enter the home and minister to the bereaved family.

So with these apostates: they make a lot of noise about things they know nothing about! The Phillips translation of 2 Peter 2:12 says they "scoff at things outside their own experience." The *New International Version* reads, "But these men blaspheme in matters they do not understand." Whenever her pupils were noisy in class, one of my teachers used to say, "Empty barrels make the most noise!" And so they do!

It is sad when the media concentrates on the "big mouths" of the false teachers instead of the "still small voice" of the Lord as He ministers through those who are true to Him. It is sadder still when innocent people become fascinated by these "great swelling words of vanity" (2:18) and cannot discern between truth and propaganda. The truth of the Word of God leads to salvation, but the arrogant words of the apostates lead only to condemnation.

These "brute beasts" are destined for destruction, a truth Peter mentioned often in 2 Peter 2 (vv. 3-4, 9, 12, 17, 20). As they seek to destroy the faith, they themselves shall be destroyed. They will be "corrupted in their own corruption." Their very nature will drag them down into destruction, like the pig returning to the mire and the dog to its vomit (2:22). Unfortunately, before that event takes place, these people can do a great deal of moral and spiritual damage.

Their Reveling (2 Peter 2:13-14a)
The words translated *riot* and *sporting* carry the meaning of "sensual reveling." They also contain the idea of luxury, softness, and extravagance. At the expense of those who sup-

port them (v. 3), the apostates enjoy luxurious living. In our own society, there are those who plead for funds for their "ministries," yet live in expensive houses, drive luxury cars, and wear costly clothes. When we remember that Jesus became poor in order to make us rich, their garish lifestyle seems out of step with New Testament Christianity.

Not only do they deceive others, but they even deceive themselves! They can "prove" from the Bible that their lifestyle is right. In ancient times, it was expected that people would revel at night, but these people dared to revel in the daytime, so convinced were they of their practices. A person can become so accustomed to his vices that he sees them as virtues.

If they kept their way of life out of the church, we would not have to be as concerned—but they are a part of the fellowship! They were even sharing in the "love feasts" that the early church used to enjoy in connection with the celebration of the Lord's Supper (1 Cor. 11:20-34). It was a time when the poorer believers could enjoy a decent meal because of the generosity of the Christians who were better off economically. But the apostates only used the "love feast" as a time for displaying their wealth and impressing ignorant people who lacked discernment.

Instead of bringing blessing to the fellowship, these false teachers were "spots" and "blemishes" that defiled the assembly. Somehow their behavior at the feasts defiled others and brought disgrace to the name of the Lord. It is the Word of God that helps to remove the spots and blemishes (Eph. 5:27), but these teachers do not minister the truth of the Word. They twist Scripture to make it say what they want it to say (2 Peter 3:16).

This "unconscious defilement" is a deadly thing. The Pharisees were also guilty of it (Matt. 23:25-28). False doctrine inevitably leads to false living, and false living then encourages false doctrine. The apostate must "adjust" God's Word or change his way of life, and he is not about to change his lifestyle! So, wherever he goes, he secretly defiles people and makes it easier for them to sin. It is possible to go to a church fellowship and be defiled!

Certainly our churches need to exercise authority and practice discipline. Christian love does not mean that we tolerate every false doctrine and every so-called "lifestyle." The Bible makes it clear that some things are right and some things are wrong. No Christian whose belief and behavior are contrary to the Word of God should be permitted to share in the Lord's Supper or to have a spiritual ministry in the church. His defiling influence may not be seen immediately, but ultimately it will create serious problems.

Second Peter 2:14 makes it clear that the apostates attend these church meetings for two reasons: first, to satisfy their own lusts; second, to capture converts for their cause.

They keep their eyes open, looking for "loose women" whom they can entice into sin. Paul warned about similar apostates who "creep into houses and lead captive silly women laden with sins, led away with divers lusts" (2 Tim. 3:6). More than one "minister" has used religion as a cloak to cover his own lusts. Some women, in particular, are vulnerable in "counseling sessions," and these men take advantage of them.

In one of the churches I pastored, I noticed that a young man in the choir was doing his utmost to appear a "spiritual giant" to the other choir members, especially the younger women. He prayed with fervency and often talked about his walk with the Lord. Some of the people were impressed by him, but I felt that something was wrong and that danger was in the air. Sure enough, he began to date one of the fine young ladies who happened to be a new believer. In spite of my warnings, she continued the friendship, which ended in her being seduced. I praise God that she was rescued and is now faithfully serving God, but she could have avoided that terrible experience.

The satisfying of their lusts is the false teachers' main ambition: they *cannot cease from sin.* The verb suggests "they are unable to stop." Why? Because they are in bondage (2 Peter 2:18-19). The apostates consider themselves to be "free," yet they are in the most terrible kind of slavery. Whatever they touch, they defile; whoever they enlist, they enslave.

"Beguiling unstable souls" presents the picture of a fisher-man baiting a hook or a hunter baiting a trap. The same image is used in James 1:14 where James presents tempta-tion as "the baiting of the trap." Satan knows that he could never trap us unless there is some fine bait to attract us in the first place. Satan promised Eve that she and Adam would become "like gods" if they ate of the forbidden tree (Gen. 3:4-5), and they "took the bait" and were trapped.

What kind of "bait" do the apostates use to catch people? For one thing, they offer them "liberty" (2 Peter 2:19). This probably means a perversion of the grace of God, "turning the grace of our God into lasciviousness" (Jude 4). "Since you are saved by grace," they argued, "then you have the free-dom to sin. The more you sin, the more of God's grace you will experience!" Paul answered their false arguments in Ro-mans 6, a portion of Scripture that every believer ought to master.

Along with "freedom" they also bait the trap with "fulfill-ment." This is one of the "buzz words" of our generation, and it goes right along with "doing your own thing" and "having it your way." They say, "The Christian life that the church offers is old-fashioned and outdated. We have a new lifestyle that makes you feel fulfilled and helps you find your true self!" Alas, like the prodigal son, these unstable souls try to find themselves, but they end up *losing* themselves (Luke 15:11-24). In their search for fulfillment they become very self-centered and lose the opportunities for growth that come from serving others.

There can be no freedom or fulfillment apart from submission to Jesus Christ. "The purpose of life," said P.T. Forsyth, "is not to find your freedom, but to find your master." Just as a gifted musician finds freedom and fulfillment putting himself or herself under the discipline of a great artist, or an athlete under the discipline of a great coach, so the believer finds true freedom and fulfillment under the authority of Jesus Christ.

Who are the people who "take the bait" that the apostates put into their subtle traps? Peter called them "unstable souls." Stability is an important factor in a successful Christian life. Just as a child must learn to stand before he can walk or run, so the Christian must learn to "stand firm in the Lord." Paul and the other apostles sought to establish their converts in the faith (Rom. 1:11; 16:25; 1 Thes. 3:2, 13). Peter was certain that his readers were "established in the present truth" (2 Peter 1:12), but he still warned them.

Their Revolting (2 Peter 2:14b-16)

"They have abandoned the right road" is the way the Phillips translation expresses it. The apostates know the right road, the straight path that God has established, but they deliberately abandon God's way for their own. No wonder Peter called them "natural brute beasts" (2:12) and compared them to animals! (2:22) "Be ye not as the horse, or as the mule!" warned the psalmist (Ps. 32:9). The horse likes to rush ahead and the mule likes to lag behind; both can get you off the right path. Believers are sheep, and sheep need to stay close to the shepherd or they will stray.

We have already learned one reason for the apostates' godless conduct: they want to satisfy the cravings of their flesh. But there is a second reason: they are covetous and want to exploit people for personal gain. Peter mentioned this in 2 Peter 2:3 and now develops the thought. Not only is the false teacher's outlook controlled by his passions (v. 14a), but his heart is controlled by covetousness. He is in bondage to lust for pleasure and money!

In fact, he has perfected the skill of getting what he wants. "They are experts in greed" says the *New International Version*, and the Phillips translation is even more graphic: "Their technique of getting what they want is, through long practice, highly developed." They know exactly how to motivate people to give. While the true servant of God trusts the Father to meet his needs and seeks to help people grow through their giving, the apostate trusts his "fund-raising skills" and leaves people in worse shape than he found them. He knows how to exploit the unstable and the innocent.

There is certainly nothing wrong with a ministry sharing its opportunities and needs with its praying friends. My wife and I receive many publications and letters of this kind, and, quite frankly, some of them we throw away without reading. We have learned that these ministries cannot be trusted, that their dramatic appeals are not always based on fact, and that the funds donated are not always used as they should be. The other letters and publications we read carefully, pray about, discuss, and see if God would have us invest in their work. We know we cannot support every good work that God has raised up, so we try to exercise discernment, and invest in the ministries God has chosen for us.

As Peter wrote about the devious practices of these people, he could only exclaim, "Cursed children!" They were not the "blessed" children of God but the cursed children of the devil (John 8:44). They might succeed in building up their bank accounts, but in the end, at the throne of God, they would be declared bankrupt. "Depart from me, ye cursed, into everlasting fire, prepared for the devil and his angels" (Matt. 25:41). "For what is a man profited, if he shall gain the whole world, and lose his own soul?" (Matt. 16:26)

Covetousness is the insatiable desire for more—more money, more power, more prestige. The covetous heart is never satisfied. This explains why the love of money is a root of all kinds of evil (1 Tim. 6:10), for when a person craves more money, he will commit any sin to satisfy that craving. He has already broken the first two of the Ten Commandments, because money is already his god and idol. It is then a simple step to break the others—to steal, lie, commit adultery, take God's name in vain, and so on. No wonder Jesus warned, "Take heed and beware of covetousness" (Luke 12:15).

I have read that the people in North Africa have devised a clever way to catch monkeys. They make a hole in a gourd just large enough for the monkey's paw, then fill the gourd with nuts and tie it to a tree. At night, the monkey reaches into the gourd for the nuts, only to find he cannot pull his paw out of the gourd! Of course, he could let go of the nuts and escape quite easily—but he doesn't want to forfeit the nuts! He ends up being captured because of his covetousness. We might expect this kind of stupidity in a dumb animal, but certainly not in a person made in the image of God; yet it happens every day.

Peter knew his Old Testament Scriptures. He had already used Noah and Lot to illustrate his words, and in 2 Peter 2:15-16, he used the Prophet Balaam. The story of Balaam is found in Numbers 22—25; take time now to read it.

Balaam is a mysterious character, a Gentile prophet who tried to curse the Jews. Balak, the king of the Moabites, was afraid of Israel, so he turned to Balaam for help. Balaam knew it was wrong to cooperate with Balak, but his heart was covetous and he wanted the money and honor that Balak promised him. Balaam knew the truth of God and the will of God, yet he deliberately abandoned the right way and went astray. He is a perfect illustration of the apostates in their covetous practices.

From the outset, God told Balaam not to help Balak, and, at first, Balaam obeyed and sent the messengers home. But when Balak sent more princes and promised more money and honor, Balaam decided to "pray about it again" and reconsider the matter. The second time, God tested Balaam and permitted him to go with the princes. This was not God's direct will; it was His permissive will, designed to see what the prophet would do.

Balaam jumped at the chance! But when he started to go astray, God rebuked the disobedient prophet through the mouth of his donkey. How remarkable that the animals obey God, even when their masters do not! (Read Isa. 1:3.) God permitted Balaam to set up his altars and offer his sacrifices, but God did not permit him to curse Israel. Instead, God turned Balaam's curse into a blessing (Deut. 23:4-5; Neh. 13:2).

Balaam was not able to curse Israel, but he was able to tell Balak how to defeat Israel. All the Moabites had to do was invite the Jews to be "friendly neighbors" and share in their feasts (Num. 25). Instead of maintaining its separated position, Israel compromised and joined the pagan orgies of the Moabites. God had to discipline the people and thousands of them died.

You can see in Balaam the two aspects of apostasy that Peter emphasized in this chapter: sensual lust and covetousness. He loved money and he led Israel into lustful sin. He was a man who could get messages from God, yet he led people away from God! When you read his oracles, you cannot help but be impressed with his eloquence; yet he deliber-ately disobeyed God! Balaam said, "I have sinned" (Num. 22:34), but his confession was not sincere. He even prayed, "Let me die the death of the righteous" (Num. 23:10), yet he did not want to live the life of the righteous.

Because Balaam counseled Balak to seduce Israel, God saw to it that Balaam was judged. He was slain by the sword when Israel defeated the Midianites (Num. 31:8). We won-der who received all the wealth that he had "earned" by his devious ways. Peter called his hire "the wages of unrigh-teousness." This phrase reminds us of another pretender, Judas, who received "the reward of iniquity" (Acts 1:18), and who also perished in shame.

We will have more to say about Balaam when we study Jude 11, but we must not ignore the main lesson: he was a rebel against the will of God. Like the false teachers that Peter described, Balaam knew the right way, but deliberately chose the wrong way because he wanted to make money. He kept "playing with the will of God" by trying to get "a differ-ent viewpoint" (Num. 22:41; 23:13, 27). He no doubt had a true gift from God because he uttered some beautiful proph-ecies about Jesus Christ, but he prostituted that gift to base uses just to gain honor and wealth.

A bank officer approached a junior clerk and secretly asked, "If I gave you $50,000, would you help me alter the books?"

"Yes, I guess I would," the man replied.

"Would you do it for $100?"

"Of course not!" the man said. "What do you think I am, a common thief?"

"We've already determined that," said the officer. "Now we're talking about price."

The person who is covetous does have his price, and when it is met, he will do whatever is asked, even revolt against the will of God. Peter called this attitude *madness*. The word means "to be deranged, out of your mind." But Balaam thought he was doing the wise thing; after all, he was taking advantage of a situation that might never come along again. But any rebellion against God is madness and can only lead to tragedy. It was when the prodigal son "came to himself" that he realized how stupid he had been (Luke 15:17).

Peter has condemned three sins of the false teachers: their reviling, their reveling, and their revolting. All of these sins spring from pride and selfish desire. A true servant of God is humble and seeks to serve others (see the contrast in Phil. 2:20-21). The true servant of God does not think about praise or pay, because he serves God from a loving and obedient heart. He honors God and the authority that God has established in this world. In short, the true servant of God patterns himself after Jesus Christ.

In these last days there will be an abundance of false teachers pleading for support. They are gifted and experienced when it comes to deceiving people and getting their money. It is important that God's people be established in the truth, that they know how to detect when the Scriptures are being twisted and the people exploited. I thank God for agencies that help to expose "religious rackets," but there is still the need for spiritual discernment and a growing knowledge of the Word of God.

Not all of these "religious frauds" will be discovered and put out of business. But God will one day deal with all of them! Like animals, they will be "taken and destroyed" (2 Peter 2:12). They will receive "the reward of unrighteousness" (2:13) to compensate for the wages they have exploited from others. As "cursed children" (2:14) they will be banished from the presence of the Lord forever.

They are marked men and women; they will not escape.

5

False Freedom

2 Peter 2:17-22

It is a frightening fact that many people who are now zealous members of cults were at one time attending churches that at least professed to believe the Christian Gospel. They participated in the Communion service and saw the death of the Lord Jesus portrayed in the loaf and the cup. They even recited the Apostles' Creed and the Lord's Prayer. Yet today, these people will tell you that they "feel free" now that they have been "liberated" from the Christian faith.

At the same time, you will meet people who have rejected all religious faith and now profess to enjoy a new freedom. "I used to believe that stuff," they will boldly confess, "but I don't believe it anymore. I've got something better and I feel free for the first time in my life."

Freedom is a concept that is very important in today's world, yet not everybody really understands what the word means. In fact, everybody from the Communist to the "playboy" seems to have his own definition. Nobody is completely free in the sense of having the ability and the opportunity to do whatever he wants to do. For that matter, doing whatever you please is *not* freedom—it is the worst kind of bondage.

The apostates offer freedom to their converts, and this "bait" entices them to abandon the true faith and follow the false teachers. The teachers promise them liberty, but this promise is never fulfilled; the unstable converts only find themselves in terrible bondage. The freedom offered is a *false* freedom, and Peter gave three reasons that explain why it is false.

It Is Based on False Promises (2 Peter 2:17-18)

Faith is only as good as the object. A pagan may have great faith in his idol, but the idol can do nothing for him. I have a friend who put his faith in a certain investment scheme and lost almost everything. His faith was strong but the company was weak. When you put your faith in Jesus Christ, that faith will accomplish something, because God always keeps His promises. "There hath not failed one word of all His good promise" (1 Kings 8:56).

Peter uses three vivid illustrations to emphasize the emptiness of the apostates' promises.

"WELLS WITHOUT WATER" (2:17a). The Greek word actually means "a flowing spring" rather than a tranquil well. It is the word our Lord used when He ministered to the Samaritan woman (John 4:14) and that John used in describing the satisfaction the saints will experience for all eternity (Rev. 7:17; 21:6). A spring without water is not a spring at all! A well is still called a well even if the water is gone, but a spring ceases to exist if the water is not flowing.

There is in mankind an inborn thirst for reality, for God. "Thou hast made us for Thyself," said Augustine, "and our hearts are restless until they rest in Thee." People attempt to satisfy this thirst in many ways, and they end up living on substitutes. Only Jesus Christ can give inner peace and satisfaction.

"Whosoever drinketh [present tense, "keeps on drinking"] of this water [in the well] shall thirst again," said Jesus, "but whosoever drinketh [takes one drink once and for all] of the water that I shall give him shall never thirst" (John 4:13-14). What a contrast! You may drink repeatedly at the broken cisterns of the world and never find satisfaction, but you may take one drink of the Living Water through faith in Jesus Christ, and you will be satisfied forever. The false teachers could not make this kind of an offer, because they had nothing to offer. They could promise, but they could not produce.

"CLOUDS THAT ARE CARRIED WITH A TEMPEST" (2:17b). The picture is that of clouds of fog or mist being driven by a squall over a lake or sea. Clouds ought to announce the possibility of rain, but these clouds only announce that a windstorm is coming. Jude's description is, "Clouds they are without water, carried about of winds" (v. 12). Again, there is noise, motion, and something to watch, but nothing profitable happens. The farmer sees the clouds and prays they will empty rain on his parched fields. The false teachers have nothing to give; they are empty.

"THE MIST OF DARKNESS" (2:17c). The word translated *mist* means "blackness, gloom," so "the blackness of the darkness" would be an accurate translation (see v. 4). These apostates promise to lead people into the light, but they themselves end up in the darkest part of the darkness! (See Jude 6 and 13.) The atmosphere of hell is not uniform: some places will be darker than others. How tragic that innocent people will be led astray by these apostates and possibly end up in hell with them.

Since these false teachers really have nothing to give, how are they able to attract followers? The reasons are found in 2 Peter 2:18.

First, the teachers are eloquent promoters of their doctrines. They know how to impress people with their vocabulary, "inflated words that say nothing" (literal translation). The average person does not know how to listen to and analyze the kind of propaganda that pours out of the mouths and printing presses of the apostates. Many people cannot tell the difference between a religious huckster and a sincere servant of Jesus Christ.

Do not be impressed with religious oratory. Apollos was a fervent and eloquent religious speaker, but he did not know the right message to preach (Acts 18:24-28). Paul was careful not to build his converts' faith on either his words or his wisdom (1 Cor. 2:1-5). Paul was a brilliant man, but his ministry was simple and practical. He preached to *express* and not to *impress*. He knew the difference between *communication* and *manipulation*.

The second reason the apostates are so successful is that they appeal to the base appetites of the old nature. This is part of their bait! (2 Peter 2:14) We must not think of "the lusts of the flesh" only in terms of sexual sins, for the flesh has other appetites. Read the list given in Galatians 5:19-21 and you will see the many different kinds of "bait" the apostates have available for baiting their traps.

For example, *pride* is one of the sins of the flesh, and apostate teachers like to appeal to the human ego. A true servant of God will lovingly tell people that they are lost sinners, under the wrath of a holy God, but the apostate minister will try to avoid "putting people on a guilt trip." He will tell his listeners how good they are, how much God loves them *and needs them* and how easy it is to get into the family of God. In fact, he may tell them they are already in God's family and just need to start living like it! The apostate avoids talking about repentance, because egotistical men do not want to repent.

The third reason they are successful is that they appeal to immature people, people who have "very recently escaped" from their old ways. The apostate has no message for the down-and-out sinner, but he does have a message for the new believer.

A pastor friend of mine was assisting some missionaries in the Philippines by conducting open-air meetings near the university. Students who wanted to decide for Christ were asked to step into a building near the square, and there they were counseled and also given follow-up material to help them get started in their Christian life.

No sooner did a new convert walk out the door and past the crowd than a cultist would join him and start to introduce his own religion! All the apostates had to do was look for the people carrying follow-up material! This same procedure is often used in large evangelistic crusades: the false teachers are ready to pounce on new believers carrying decision packets.

This is why it is important that soul-winners, pastors, and other Christian workers ground new converts in the faith. Like newborn babies, new Christians need to be protected, fed, and established before they can be turned loose in this dangerous world. One reason Peter wrote this letter was to warn the church to care for the new Christians, because the false teachers were out to get them! We cannot blame new believers for being "unstable" (v. 14) if we have not taught them how to stand.

The freedom the apostates offer is a false freedom because it is based on false promises. There is a second reason why it is false.

It Is Offered by False Christians (2 Peter 2:19-20)
You cannot set someone free if you are in bondage yourself, and these false teachers were in bondage. Peter made it

clear that these men had temporarily disentangled themselves from the pollutions of the world, but then they went
right back into bondage again! They professed to be saved
but had never really been redeemed (set free) at all!

The tenses of the verbs in verse 19 are present: "While they
promise them [the new believers] liberty, they themselves
[the apostates] *are* the servants of corruption" (italics mine).
They claim to be the servants of God, but they are only the
servants of sin. It is bad enough to be a slave, but when sin
is your master, you are in the worst possible condition a
person can experience.

As you review what Peter has written so far, you can see
the kinds of sins that enslave the false teachers. For one
thing, they were in bondage to money (vv. 3, 14). Their
covetousness forced them to use every kind of deceptive technique to exploit innocent people. They were also in bondage
to fleshly lust (vv. 10, 14). They had their eyes on weak
women whom they could seduce. (In view of what Peter and
Jude wrote about Sodom and Gomorrah, perhaps we should
also include weak men and boys.)

They were also enslaved by pride (vv. 10-12). They
thought nothing of speaking evil of those in places of authority, including the angels and God! They promoted themselves
and derided everybody else. Sad to say, there are people who
admire this kind of arrogance, who follow these proud men
and support them.

It is interesting to compare the three men Peter named in
this chapter—Noah, Lot, and Balaam. Noah kept himself
completely separated from the apostasy of the world of his
day. He boldly preached God's righteousness and was faithful in his walk and witness, even though no one but his
family followed the Lord.

Lot knew the truth and kept himself pure, but he did not
keep himself separated; he lost his family as a result. Lot

hated the wickedness of Sodom, yet he lived in the midst of it and, by doing so, exposed his daughters and wife to god-less influences.

Balaam not only followed the ways of sin, but he encour-aged other people to sin! He told Balak how to seduce the nation Israel and his plan almost succeeded. Lot lost his family, but Balaam lost his life.

Beware of "the deceitfulness of sin" (Heb. 3:13). Sin always promises freedom but in the end brings bondage. It promises life but instead brings death. Sin has a way of gradually binding a person until there is no way of escape, apart from the gracious intervention of the Lord. Even the bondage that sin creates is deceitful, for the people who are bound actually think they are free! Too late they discover that they are prisoners of their own appetites and habits.

Jesus Christ came to bring freedom. In His first sermon in the synagogue at Nazareth, our Lord sounded forth the trumpet call of freedom and the advent of the "Year of Jubilee" (Luke 4:16ff). But Christ's *meaning* of freedom is different from the apostates' as is His method for accomp-lishing it.

In the Bible, freedom does not mean "doing your own thing" or "having it your way." That attitude is the very essence of sin. The freedom that Jesus Christ offers means *enjoying fulfillment in the will of God.* It means achieving your greatest potential to the glory of God. The Quaker lead-er Rufus Jones, paraphrasing Aristotle, said, "The true nature of a thing is the highest that it can become." Jesus Christ frees us to become our very best in this life, and then to be like Him in the next.

The apostates brought their followers into bondage by means of lies, but our Lord brings us into freedom by means of truth. "And ye shall know the truth, and the truth shall make you free" (John 8:32). He was speaking, of course, about the truth of the Word of God. "Sanctify them through Thy truth," He prayed; "Thy Word is truth" (John 17:17). Through the Word of God, we discover the truth about ourselves, our world, and our God. As we face this truth honestly, we experience the liberating power of the Spirit of God. We cease living in a world of fantasy and enter a world of reality, and through the power of God, we are able to fulfill His will, grow in grace, and "reign in life by one, Jesus Christ" (Rom. 5:17).

Those who live by God's truth enter into more and more freedom, but those who live by lies experience more and more bondage, until "the latter end is worse with them than the beginning" (2 Peter 2:20). This reminds us of our Lord's parable in Matthew 12:43-45, the truth of which parallels what Peter has written. *Temporary reformation without true repentance and rebirth only leads to greater sin and judgment.* Reformation cleans up the outside, but regeneration changes the inside.

Sinful tendencies do not disappear when a person reforms; they merely hibernate *and get stronger.* Holiness is not simply refusing to do evil things, for even unsaved people can practice self-control. True holiness is more than conquering temptation: it is conquering even *the desire* to disobey God. When my doctor told me to lose weight, he said, "I'll tell you how to do it: learn to hate the things that aren't good for you." His advice worked!

You can expect nothing but "false freedom" from false Christians who offer false promises. But there is a third reason why this freedom is false.

It Involves a False Experience (2 Peter 2:21-22)

Peter called these apostates "natural brute beasts" (v. 12), and then ended the warning by describing them as pigs and dogs! But he was not simply showing his personal disdain for them; rather, he was teaching a basic spiritual lesson.

It is very important that we understand that the pronoun *they* in this entire paragraph (vv. 17-22) refers to the false teachers and not to their converts. It is also important that we remember that these teachers are not truly born-again people. Jude described these same people in his letter and stated clearly that they were "sensual, having not the Spirit" (v. 19). It is not *profession* of spirituality that marks a true believer but *possession* of the Spirit of God within (Rom. 8:9).

But these apostates did have a "religious experience"! And they would boldly claim that their experience brought them into fellowship with the Lord. They would be able to explain "the way of righteousness," and would use the Word of God to support their teachings. If they had not experienced some kind of "religious conversion," they would never have been able to get into the fellowship of the local assemblies.

But their experience, like their promises, was false.

Since Peter wrote both of his letters to the same group of believers we may assume that they had the doctrinal foundation presented so clearly in his first letter. Peter emphasized the new birth (1 Peter 1:3, 22-25). He reminded his readers that they were "partakers of the divine nature" (2 Peter 1:4). In his first letter, Peter described the believers as sheep (1 Peter 2:25; 5:1-4). Our Lord used this same image when He reinstated Peter into the apostleship after his denials (John 21:15-17).

There is no indication that the false teachers had ever experienced the new birth. They had *knowledge* of salvation and could use the language of the church, but they lacked that true saving experience with the Lord. At one time they had even received the Word of God (2 Peter 2:21), but then they turned away from it. *They never trusted Christ and became His sheep.*

Instead of being sheep, they were pigs and dogs—and keep in mind that the dogs in that day were not pampered pets! The Jews called the Gentiles "dogs" because a dog was nothing but a filthy scavenger who lived on garbage! It was hardly a title of respect and endearment!

These men could point to "an experience," but it was a *false* experience. Satan is the counterfeiter. We have already seen that Satan has a false Gospel (Gal. 1:6-9), preached by false ministers (2 Cor. 11:13-15), producing false Christians (2 Cor. 11:26—"in perils among false brethren"). In His Parable of the Tares, our Lord taught that Satan plants his counterfeits ("the children of the wicked one") wherever God plants true believers (Matt. 13:24-30, 36-43).

What kind of "experience" did these false teachers have? To use Peter's vivid images, the pig was washed on the outside, but remained a pig; the dog was "cleaned up" on the inside, but remained a dog. The pig *looked* better and the dog *felt* better, but neither one had been changed. They each had the same old nature, not a new one.

This explains why both animals returned to the old life: it was part of their nature. A pig can stay clean only a short time and then must head for the nearest mudhole. We do not condemn a pig for acting like a pig because it has a pig's nature. If we saw *a sheep* heading for the mire, we would be concerned!

When I was a youngster, one of our neighbors owned a scrubby black mutt with the imaginative name of "Blackie." He had the habit of eating what dogs should not eat, and then regurgitating somewhere in the neighborhood, usually on our sidewalk. But that was not all. Blackie would then return to the scene of the crime and start all over again! Apparently dogs have been doing this for centuries, for Solomon mentioned it in Proverbs 26:11, the text that Peter quoted.

Certainly the dog feels better after emptying his stomach, *but it is still a dog.* "Having an experience" did not change his nature. Quite the contrary, it only gave further evidence of his "dog nature," because he came back and (just like a dog) lapped up his own vomit. It is a disgusting picture, but that is exactly the response Peter wanted to produce.

In my ministry, I have met people who have told me about their "spiritual experiences," but in their narratives I detected no evidence of a new nature. Like the sow, some of them were cleaned up on the outside. Like the dog, some of them were cleaned up temporarily on the inside and actually felt better. But in no case had they become "partakers of the divine nature" (2 Peter 1:4). They thought they were free from their problems and sins, when really they were still in bondage to an old sinful nature.

According to 2 Peter 2:20, these apostates "escaped the pollutions of the world." Pollution is defilement on the outside. But true believers have "escaped the corruption that is in the world through [because of] lust" (1:4). Corruption is much deeper than defilement on the outside: it is decay on the inside. True believers have received a new nature, a divine nature, and they have new and different appetites and desires. They have been transformed from pigs and dogs into sheep!

Imagine the disappointment of the person who thinks he has been delivered, only to discover that, in the end, he is in worse shape than when he started! The apostates promise freedom, but all they can give is bondage. True freedom must come from within; it has to do with the inner nature of the person. Because the true nature of a thing is the highest that it can become, a pig and dog can never rise higher than *Sus scrofa* and *Canis familiaris.*

I realize that there are some who believe that these apostate teachers were true believers who, in turning from the knowledge of Christ, forfeited their salvation. Even a casual reading of 2 Peter 2 and Jude would convince the impartial reader that these teachers never had a true experience of salvation through faith in Jesus Christ. Peter would never have compared them to swine and dogs had they once been members of the Lord's true flock, nor would he have called them "cursed children" (2:14). If they were true believers who had gone astray, it would have been Peter's responsibility to encourage his readers to rescue these backsliders (James 5:19-20), but Peter did not command them to do so. Instead, he condemned the apostates in some of the most forceful language found in the New Testament!

Now we better understand why this "freedom" offered by these teachers is a *false* freedom, a "freedom" that only leads to bondage. It is based on false promises, empty words that sound exciting but that have no divine authority behind them. It is offered by false Christians who were involved in a false experience. From start to finish, this "freedom" is the product of our adversary, the devil!

Now we can appreciate Peter's admonition in 2 Peter 1:10—"Wherefore the rather, brethren, give diligence to make your calling and election sure." In other words, "Has your spiritual experience been genuine?" It is a startling fact that there are many people in our churches who have never truly been born again, but who are convinced that they are saved and going to heaven! They have had "an experience," and perhaps look better (like the sow) and feel better (like the dog), but they have not been *made better* as "partakers of the divine nature."

Perhaps Peter recalled Judas, one of the Twelve, who was a tool of the devil and was never born again. Up to the very end, the other disciples did not know the truth about Judas and thought he was a spiritual man!

The apostates appear to have successful ministries, but in

the end, they are bound to fail.

The important thing is that you and I have the assurance of a true experience with the Lord, and that we have nothing to do with these counterfeit ministries, no matter how popular they may be.

Christ is "the truth" (John 14:6) and following Him leads to freedom. The apostates are liars and following them leads to bondage. There can be no middle ground!

6

Scoffing
at the Scoffers

2 Peter 3:1-10

"Everybody is ignorant," said Will Rogers, "only on different subjects."

How true, and yet that is not the whole story because there is more than one kind of ignorance. Some people are ignorant because of lack of opportunity to learn, or perhaps lack of ability to learn; others are (to use Peter's phrase in 2 Peter 3:5) "willingly . . . ignorant." "Not ignorance, but ignorance of ignorance, is the death of knowledge," said a famous philosopher, and he is right.

Peter has dealt with the character and conduct of the apostates in 2 Peter 2, and now he deals with their false teaching. Peter affirmed the certainty of Christ's coming in glory (1:16ff), a truth that the apostates questioned and denied. In fact, they were scoffing at the very idea of the return of the Lord, the judgment of the world, and the establishment of a glorious kingdom.

How important it is for us as Christians to understand God's truth! Today we are surrounded by scoffers, people who refuse to take the Bible seriously when it speaks about

Christ's return and the certainty of judgment. In this paragraph, Peter admonished his readers to understand three important facts about God and the promise of Christ's coming.

God's Word Is True (2 Peter 3:1-4)

It is possible to have a pure and sincere mind and yet have a bad memory! Peter wrote this second letter primarily to awaken and arouse his readers (1:12-15). It is easy for Christians to "get accustomed to God's truth." Eutychus went to sleep listening to Paul preach! (Acts 20:7-10) Our heavenly Father sacrificed so that we might have the truth of the Word and the freedom to practice it, but too often we take this for granted and become complacent. The church needs to be aroused regularly lest the enemy find us asleep and take advantage of our spiritual lethargy.

Because God's Word is true, we must pay attention to it and take its message seriously. New converts must be taught the Word and established in the doctrines of the faith, for new Christians are the apostate teacher's primary targets. But older Christians must also be reminded of the importance of Bible doctrine and, in particular, the doctrines that relate to the return of Christ. Prophetic teaching must not lull us to sleep. Rather, it must awaken us to live godly lives and to seek to win the lost (Rom. 13:11-14).

What the Bible teaches about the Day of the Lord was not invented by the apostles. The prophets taught it and so did our Lord Jesus Christ (2 Peter 3:2). Peter emphasized the *unity* of the Word of God. When the scoffers denied "the power and coming" of Jesus Christ, they were denying the truth of the prophetic books, the teaching of our Lord in the Gospels, and the writing of the apostles! Like our Lord's seamless garment, the Scriptures cannot be cut apart without ruining the whole.

As far back as the days of Enoch, God warned that judgment was coming (Jude 14-15). Many of the Hebrew prophets announced the Day of the Lord and warned that the world would be judged (Isa. 2:10-22; 13:6-16; Jer. 30:7; Dan. 12:1; the Book of Joel; Amos 5:18-20; the Book of Zephaniah; Zech. 12:1—14:3). This period of judgment is also known as "the time of Jacob's trouble" (Jer. 30:7) and the Tribulation.

Our Lord taught about this day of judgment in His sermon on the Mount of Olives (Matt. 24—25). Paul discussed it in 1 Thessalonians 5 and 2 Thessalonians 1—2. The Apostle John described this terrible day in Revelation 6—19. It will be a time when God's wrath will be poured out on the nations, and when Satan will be free to give vent to his anger and malice. It will culminate with the return of Jesus Christ in glory and victory.

While I do not make it a test of fellowship or spirituality, I personally believe that the people of God will be taken to heaven *before* this "great and terrible day" dawns.

I think we should carefully distinguish the various "days" mentioned in the Bible. "The Day of the Lord" is that day of judgment that climaxes with the return of Christ to the earth. "The Day of God" (2 Peter 3:12) is the period when God's people enjoy the new heavens and the new earth, when all evil has been judged (1 Cor. 15:28). "The Day of Christ" relates to the coming of Christ for His church (1 Cor. 1:7-9; Phil. 1:10; 2:16).

Prophetic students seem to fall into three categories: those who believe the church will be raptured ("caught up together," 1 Thes. 4:13ff) *before* the Day of the Lord; those who see this event taking place *in the middle of* the Day of the Lord, so that the church experiences the first half of the Tribulation; and those who believe the church will be raptured when the Lord returns *at the Tribulation's close*. There are good and godly people in each group and our differences of interpretation must not create problems in fellowship or in sharing Christian love.

Not only does the Word of God predict the coming Day of the Lord, but it also predicts the appearance of the very scoffers who deny that Word! Their presence is proof that the Word they deny is the true Word of God! We should not be surprised at the presence of these apostate mockers (see Acts 20:28-31; 1 Tim. 4; 2 Tim. 3).

A scoffer is someone who treats lightly that which ought to be taken seriously. The people in Noah's day scoffed at the idea of a judgment, and the citizens of Sodom scoffed at the possibility of fire and brimstone destroying their sinful city. If you have tried at all to witness for Jesus Christ, you have no doubt met people who scoff at the idea of hell or a future day of judgment for this world.

Why do these apostates scoff? Because they want to continue living in their sins. Peter made it clear that false teachers cultivate "the lust of uncleanness" (2 Peter 2:10) and allure weak people by means of "the lusts of the flesh" (2:18). If your lifestyle contradicts the Word of God, you must either change your lifestyle or change the Word of God. The apostates choose the latter approach, so they scoff at the doctrines of judgment and the coming of the Lord.

What is their argument? The uniformity of the world. "Nothing cataclysmic has happened in the past," they argue, "so there is no reason to believe it will happen in the future." They take the "scientific approach" by examining evidence, applying reason, and drawing a conclusion. The fact that they *willfully ignore* a good deal of evidence does not seem to disturb them.

The scientific approach works admirably in matters that relate to the material universe, but you cannot take Bible prophecy into a laboratory and treat it as though it were another hypothesis. For that matter, the so-called "laws of science" are really only educated conclusions based on a limited number of experiments and tests. These laws are generalizations, always subject to change, because no scientist can perform an infinite number of experiments to prove his claim. Nor can he completely control all the factors involved in the experiments and in his own thinking.

The Word of God is still "a light that shineth in a dark [squalid] place" (1:19). We can trust it. No matter what the scoffers may claim, God's day of judgment will come on the world, and Jesus Christ shall return to establish His glorious kingdom.

God's Work Is Consistent (2 Peter 3:5-7)

How did Peter refute the foolish argument of the apostate scoffers? "God does not interrupt the operation of His stable creation!" they argued. "The promise of Christ's coming is not true!" All Peter did was remind them of what God had done in the past and thus prove that His work is consistent throughout the ages. Peter simply presented evidence that the false teachers *deliberately* ignored. It is amazing how so-called "thinkers" (scientists, liberal theologians, philosophers) will be *selective* and deliberately refuse to consider certain data.

Peter cited two events in history to prove his point: the work of God at Creation (3:5), and the flood in Noah's day (3:6).

God created the heavens and the earth by His Word. The phrase "and God said" occurs nine times in Genesis 1. "For He spake, and it was done; He commanded, and it stood fast" (Ps. 33:9). Not only was Creation *made* by the Word of God, but it was *held together* by that same Word. Kenneth Wuest translates 2 Peter 3:5 to bring out this subtle meaning: "For concerning this they willfully forget that heavens existed from ancient times, and land [standing] out of water, and by means of water cohering by the Word of God."

Peter's argument is obvious: the same God who created the world by His Word can also intervene in His world and do whatever He wishes to do! It is His Word that made it and that holds it together, and His Word is all-powerful.

The second event Peter cited was Noah's flood (3:6). He had already referred to the Flood as an illustration of divine judgment (2:5), so there was no need to go into detail. The Flood was a cataclysmic event; in fact, the Greek word translated *overflowed* gives us our English word *cataclysm*. The people living on earth had probably never seen a rainstorm or the fountains of the deep broken up, but these events happened just the same. Their "scientists" could have argued as the scoffers argued, "Everything goes on as it did from the beginning. Life is uniform so nothing unusual can happen." But it happened!

God has the power to "break in" at any time and accomplish His will. He can send rain from heaven or fire from heaven. "But our God is in the heavens: He hath done whatsoever He hath pleased" (Ps. 115:3).

Having established the fact that God has in the past "interrupted" the course of history, Peter was then ready for his application in 2 Peter 2:7. The same Word that created and sustains the world is now holding it together, stored with fire, being preserved and reserved for that future day of judgment. God promised that there would be no more floods to destroy the world (Gen. 9:8-17). The next judgment will be a judgment of fire.

The phrase "stored with fire" used by Kenneth Wuest ("reserved unto fire," KJV) sounds very modern. Modern atomic science has revealed that the elements that make up the world are stored with power. There is enough atomic energy in a glass of water to run a huge ocean liner. Man has discovered this great power and, as a result, the world seems to teeter on the brink of atomic destruction. However, Peter seems to indicate that *man* will not destroy the world by his sinful abuse of atomic energy. It is *God* who will "push the button" at the right time and burn up the old creation and all the works of sinful man with it; then He will usher in the new heavens and earth and reign in glory.

Everything in God's original creation was good. It is man's sin that has turned a good creation into a *groaning* creation (Rom. 8:18-22). God could not permit sinful man to live in a perfect environment, so He had to curse the ground because of man (Gen. 3:14-19). Since that time, man has been busy polluting and destroying God's creation. For years, it appeared that this exploitation would not cause too much trouble, but now we are changing our minds. The balance of nature has been upset; valuable resources have been wasted; the supply of energy is running down; and civilization is facing a crisis. The prophets of doom today are not only preachers and evangelists, but also sociologists, ecologists, and atomic scientists.

Peter proved his point: God is able to intervene in the course of history. He did it in the past and He is able to do it again. The Day of the Lord that was promised by the prophets and apostles, as well as by Jesus Christ, will come just as surely as the flood came in Noah's day and the fire and brimstone came to destroy Sodom and Gomorrah.

But the scoffers had their argument ready: "Then why the delay?" The promise of Christ's coming and the judgment of the world has been around for centuries, and it is yet to be fulfilled. Has God changed His mind? The world today is certainly ripe for judgment! Thus, Peter's third fact:

God's Will Is Merciful (2 Peter 3:8-10)
Once again, Peter exposed the ignorance of the scoffers. Not only were they ignorant of what God had done in the past

(v. 5), but they were also ignorant of what God was like. They were making God in their own image and ignoring the fact that God is eternal. This means that He has neither beginning nor ending. Man is immortal: he has a beginning but not an ending. He will live forever either in heaven or hell. But God is eternal, without beginning or ending, and He dwells in eternity. Eternity is not just "extended time." Rather, it is existence *above and apart from time*.

Peter was certainly referring to Psalm 90:4—"For a thousand years in Thy sight are but as yesterday when it is past, and as a watch in the night." Isaac Watts used Psalm 90 as the basis for the familiar hymn, "O God, Our Help in Ages Past."

> A thousand ages, in Thy sight
> Are like an evening gone;
> Short as the watch that ends the night,
> Before the rising sun.

Since a thousand years are as one day to the Lord, we cannot accuse Him of delayed fulfillment of His promises. In God's sight, the whole universe is only a few days old! He is not limited by time the way we are, nor does He measure it according to man's standards. When you study the works of God, especially in the Old Testament, you can see that He is never in a hurry, but He is never late.

He could have created the entire universe in an instant, yet He preferred to do it over a period of six days. He could have delivered Israel from Egypt in a moment, yet He preferred to invest eighty years in training Moses. For that matter, He could have sent the Saviour much sooner, but He waited until "the fullness of the time was come" (Gal. 4:4). While God works *in* time, He is not limited *by* time.

To God, a thousand years is as one day, and one day as a

thousand years. God can accomplish in one day what it would take others a millennium to accomplish! He waits to work, but once He begins to work, He gets things done!

The scoffers did not understand God's eternality nor did they understand His mercy. Why was God delaying the return of Christ and the coming of the Day of the Lord? It was not because He was *unable* to act or *unwilling* to act. He was not tardy or off schedule! Nobody on earth has the right to decide when God must act. God is sovereign in all things and does not need prodding or even counsel from sinful man (Rom. 11:33-36).

God delays the coming of Christ and the great day of fiery judgment because He is long-suffering and wants to give lost sinners the opportunity to be saved. "And account that the long-suffering of our Lord is salvation" (2 Peter 3:15).

God's "delay" is actually an indication that He has a plan for this world and that He is working His plan. There should be no question in anybody's mind whether God *wants* sinners to be saved. God "is not willing that any should perish" (3:9). First Timothy 2:4 affirms that God "will have all men to be saved, and to come unto the knowledge of the truth." These verses give both the negative and the positive, and together they assure us that God has no pleasure in the death of the wicked (Ezek. 18:23, 32; 33:11). He shows His mercy to all (Rom. 11:32) even though not all will be saved.

It is worth noting that God revealed this same long-suffering in the years before the Flood (1 Peter 3:20). He saw the violence and wickedness of man and could have judged the world immediately; yet He held back His wrath and, instead, sent Noah as a "preacher of righteousness." In the case of Sodom and Gomorrah, God patiently waited while Abraham interceded for the cities and He would have spared them had He found ten righteous people in Sodom.

If God is long-suffering toward lost sinners, why did Peter

write, "The Lord . . . is long-suffering to us-ward"? Who is meant by "us-ward"? It would appear that God is long-suffering *to His own people!*

Perhaps Peter was using the word *us* in a general way, meaning "mankind." But it is more likely that he was referring to his readers as the elect of God (1 Peter 1:2; 2 Peter 1:10). God is long-suffering toward lost sinners because some of them *will* believe and become a part of God's elect people. We do not know who God's elect are among the unsaved people of the world, nor are we supposed to know. Our task is to make our *own* "calling and election sure" (1:10; cf. Luke 13:23-30). The fact that God has His elect people is an encouragement to us to share the Good News and seek to win others to Christ.

God was even long-suffering toward the scoffers of that day! They needed to repent and He was willing to save them. This is the only place where Peter used the word *repentance* in either of his letters, but that does not minimize its importance. To repent simply means "to change one's mind." It is not "regret," which usually means "being sorry I got caught." Nor is it "remorse," which is a hopeless attitude that can lead to despair.

Repentance is a change of mind that results in an action of the will. If the sinner honestly changes his mind about sin, he will turn from it. If he sincerely changes his mind about Jesus Christ, he will turn to Him, trust Him, and be saved. "Repentance toward God, and faith toward our Lord Jesus Christ" (Acts 20:21) is God's formula for salvation.

The word translated *come* at the end of 2 Peter 3:9 carries the meaning of "make room for." It is translated *contain* in John 2:6 and 21:25. The lost sinner needs to "make room" for repentance in his heart by putting away his pride and meekly receiving the Word of God. Repentance is a gift from God (Acts 11:18; 2 Tim. 2:25), but the unbeliever must make room for the gift.

As you review Peter's arguments, you can see that his evidence is irrefutable. He pointed out that the scoffers willfully rejected evidence in order that they might continue in their sins and scoffing. He proved from the Scriptures that God has intervened in past history, and that He has the power to do it today. He showed that the scoffers had a very low view of God's character because they thought He delayed in keeping His promises just as men do. Finally, he explained that God does not live in the realm of human time, and that His so-called "delay" only gives more opportunity for lost sinners to repent and be saved.

Having refuted their false claims, Peter then reaffirmed the certainty of the coming of the Day of the Lord. When will it come? Nobody knows when, because it will come to the world "as a thief in the night." Our Lord used this phrase (Matt. 24:43; Luke 12:39) and so did the Apostle Paul (1 Thes. 5:2ff). When the world is feeling secure, then God's judgment will fall. The thief does not warn his victims that he is coming! "For when they shall say, 'Peace and safety'; then sudden destruction cometh upon them, as travail upon a woman with child; and they shall not escape" (1 Thes. 5:3).

We do not know *when* it will happen, but we are told *what* will happen. Kenneth Wuest gives an accurate and graphic translation of these words: "In which the heavens with a rushing noise will be dissolved, and the elements being scorched will be dissolved, and the earth also and the works in it will be burned up" (2 Peter 3:10).

Many Bible students believe that Peter here described the action of atomic energy being released by God. The word translated *a great noise* in the *King James Version* means "with a hissing and a crackling sound." When the atomic bomb was tested in the Nevada desert, more than one reporter said that the explosion gave forth "a whirring sound," or a "crackling sound." The Greek word Peter used was commonly used by the people for the whirring of a bird's wings or the hissing of a snake.

The word *melt* in verse 10 means "to disintegrate, to be dissolved." It carries the idea of something being broken down into its basic elements, and that is what happens when atomic energy is released. "Heaven and earth shall pass away," said our Lord (Matt. 24:35), and it appears that this may happen by the release of the atomic power stored in the elements that make up the world. The heavens and earth are "stored with fire" (2 Peter 3:7, WUEST), and only God can release it.

For this reason, I do not personally believe that God will permit sinful men to engage in an earth-destroying atomic war. He will, I believe, overrule the ignorance and foolishness of men including well-meaning but unbelieving diplomats and politicians, so that He alone will have the privilege of "pushing the button" and dissolving the elements to make way for a new heaven and a new earth. Peter no doubt had in mind Old Testament passages such as Isaiah 13:10-11, 24:19, 34:4, and 64:1-4 when he wrote these words. The first passage is especially emphatic that *God* will bring judgment and not sinful man. "And I will punish the world for their evil, and the wicked for their iniquity," says the Lord. It does not sound as though He will give this task to some nervous military leader or some angry politician.

Of course, this great explosion and conflagration will not touch the "heaven of heavens" where God dwells. It will destroy the earth and the atmospheric heavens around it, the universe as we know it; this will make room for the new heavens and earth (2 Peter 3:13; Rev. 21:1ff).

Man's great works will also be burned up! All of the things that man boasts about—his great cities, his great buildings, his inventions, his achievements—will be destroyed in a moment of time. When sinners stand before the throne of God, they will have nothing to point to as evidence of their greatness. It will all be gone.

This is certainly a solemn truth, and we dare not study it in cavalier fashion. In the remaining verses of this letter, Peter will apply this truth to our daily living. But it would be wise for us to pause now and consider: where will I be when God destroys the world? Is what I am living for only destined to go up in an atomic cloud, to vanish forever? Or am I doing the will of God so that my works will glorify Him forever?

Make your decision now—before it is too late.

7

Be Diligent!

2 Peter 3:11-18

The purpose of prophetic truth is not speculation but motivation; thus Peter concluded his letter with the kind of practical admonitions that all of us must heed. It is unfortunate when people run from one prophetic conference to another, filling their notebooks, marking their Bibles, drawing their charts, and yet not living their lives to the glory of God. In fact, some of the saints battle each other more over prophetic interpretation than perhaps any other subject.

All true Christians believe that Jesus Christ is coming again. They may differ in their views of when certain promised events will occur, but they all agree that He is returning as He promised. Furthermore, all Christians agree that this faith in future glory ought to motivate the church. As one pastor said to me, "I have moved off the Program Committee and joined the Welcoming Committee!" This does not mean that we should stop studying prophecy, or that every opposing viewpoint is correct, which is an impossibility. But it does mean that, whatever views we hold, they ought to make a difference in our lives.

"Be diligent!" is the admonition that best summarizes what Peter wrote in this closing paragraph. He used this word before in 2 Peter 1: "Giving all diligence, add to your faith" (v. 5); "Give diligence to make your calling and election sure" (v. 10); "Moreover I will endeavor [be diligent] that ye may be able" (v. 15). If we are going to be successful Christians, we must learn to be diligent.

Peter gave three admonitions to encourage the readers in Christian diligence in the light of our Lord's return.

Be Diligent to Live Godly Lives (2 Peter 3:11-14)

The key word in this paragraph is *look*. It means "to await eagerly, to be expectant." You find it in Luke 3:15 ("And as the people were in expectation") and Acts 3:5 ("expecting to receive something of them"). It describes an attitude of excitement and expectation as we wait for the Lord's return. Because we realize that the world and its works will be dissolved, and that even the very elements will be disintegrated, we fix our hope, not on anything in this world, but only on the Lord Jesus Christ.

Because we do not know the day or the hour of our Lord's return, we must constantly be ready. The believer who starts to neglect the "blessed hope" (Titus 2:13) will gradually develop a cold heart, a worldly attitude, and an unfaithful life (Luke 12:35-48). If he is not careful, he may even become like the scoffers and laugh at the promise of Christ's coming.

This expectant attitude ought to make a difference in our *personal conduct* (2 Peter 3:11). The word translated *manner* literally means "exotic, out of this world, foreign." Because we have "escaped the corruption that is in the world" (1:4), we must live differently from the people in the world. To them, we should behave like "foreigners." Why? Because this world is not our home! We are "strangers and pilgrims" (1 Peter 2:11) headed for a better world, the eternal city of

God. Christians should be different, not odd. When you are different, you attract people; when you are odd, you repel them.

Our conduct should be characterized by holiness and godliness. "But as He which hath called you is holy, so be ye holy in all manner of conversation [behavior]; because it is written, 'Be ye holy; for I am holy' " (1 Peter 1:15-16). The word *holy* means "to separate, to cut off." Israel was a "holy nation" because God called the Jews out from among the Gentiles and kept them separated. Christians are called out from the godless world around them and are set apart for God alone.

The word *godliness* could be translated "piety." It is the same word we met in 2 Peter 1:6-7, "to worship well." It describes a person whose life is devoted to pleasing God. It is possible to be separated from sin positionally and yet not enjoy living for God personally. In the Greek world, the word translated *godliness* meant "respect and awe for the gods and the world they made." It is that attitude of reverence that says with John the Baptist, "He must increase, but I must decrease" (John 3:30).

Other New Testament writers also teach that an eager expectancy of the Lord's return ought to motivate us to live pure lives (see Rom. 13:11-14; 2 Cor. 5:1-11; Phil. 3:17-21; 1 Thes. 5:1-11; Titus 2:11-15; 1 John 2:28—3:3). However, it is not simply knowing the doctrine *in the mind* that motivates the life; it is having it *in the heart*, loving His appearing (2 Tim. 4:8).

Not only should this expectant attitude make a difference in our conduct, but it should also make a difference in our *witness*. The phrase *looking for and hasting unto* can be translated "looking for and hastening the coming of the Day of God." Peter affirms that it is possible for us to hasten the return of Jesus Christ.

The word translated *hasten unto* means "hasten" in the other five places where it is used in the New Testament. The shepherds "came with haste" (Luke 2:16). Jesus told Zaccheus to "make haste and come down" and "he made haste and came down" (Luke 19:5-6). Paul "hasted . . . to be at Jerusalem" (Acts 20:16); and the Lord told Paul to "make haste and get . . . out of Jerusalem" (Acts 22:18). To make this word a synonym for "eager anticipation" is to have Peter repeat himself in 2 Peter 2:12, for that is what the word *looking* means.

There are two extremes in ministry that we must avoid. One is the attitude that we are "locked into" God's sovereign plan in such a way that nothing we do will make any difference. The other extreme is to think that God cannot get anything done unless we do it! While God's sovereign decrees must never become an excuse for laziness, neither must our plans and activities try to take their place.

Perhaps two illustrations from Old Testament history will help us better understand the relationship between God's plans and man's service. God delivered Israel from Egypt and told the people He wanted to put them into their inheritance, the land of Canaan. But at Kadesh-Barnea all except Moses, Joshua, and Caleb rebelled against God and refused to enter the land (Num. 13—14). Did God force them to go in? No. Instead, He had them wander in the wilderness for the next forty years while the older generation died off. He adjusted His plan to their response.

When Jonah preached to the people of Nineveh, his message was clear: "Yet forty days, and Nineveh shall be overthrown!" (Jonah 3:4) It was God's plan to destroy the wicked city, but when the people repented, from the king on down, God adjusted His plan and spared the city. Neither God nor His basic principles changed, but His application of those principles changed. God responds when men repent.

How, then, can we as Christians hasten the coming of the Day of God? For one thing, we can pray as Jesus taught us, "Thy kingdom come" (Matt. 6:10). It would appear from Revelation 5:8 and 8:3-4 that the prayers of God's people are related in some way to the pouring out of God's wrath on the nations.

If God's work today is calling out a people for His name (Acts 15:14), then the sooner the church is completed, the sooner our Lord will return. There is a suggestion of this truth in Acts 3:19-21. While Matthew 24:14 relates primarily to the Tribulation, the principle is the same: man's ministry cooperates with God's program so that promised events can take place.

There are mysteries here that our minds cannot fully understand or explain, but the basic lesson is clear: the same God who ordains the end also ordains the means to the end, and we are a part of that means. Our task is not to speculate but to serve.

Finally, this expectant attitude will make a difference *when we meet Jesus Christ* (2 Peter 3:14). It will mean that He will greet us "in peace" and have no charges against us so that we are "ashamed before Him at His coming" (1 John 2:28). The Judgment Seat of Christ will be a serious event (2 Cor. 5:8-11) as we give an account of our service to Him (Rom. 14:10-13). It is better to meet Him "in peace" than for Him to fight against us with His Word! (Rev. 2:16)

If we are diligent to watch for His return, and to live holy and godly lives, then we will not be afraid or ashamed. We will meet Him "without spot and blameless." Jesus Christ is "a lamb without blemish and without spot" (1 Peter 1:19), and we should be careful to follow His example. Peter had warned his readers against the defilement that the apostates bring: "Spots they are and blemishes" (2 Peter 2:13). The separated Christian will not permit himself to be "spotted and blemished" by the false teachers! He wants to meet his Lord wearing pure garments.

How do we maintain this eager expectancy that leads to holy living? By keeping "His promise" before our hearts (3:13). The promise of His coming is the light that shines in this dark world (1:19), and we must be sure that "the day star" is aglow in our hearts because we love His appearing.

Be Diligent to Win the Lost (2 Peter 3:15-16)

Verse 15 ties in with verse 9, where Peter explained why the Lord had delayed fulfilling His promise. God had every reason long ago to judge the world and burn up its works, but in His mercy, He is long-suffering with us, "not willing that any should perish, but that all should come to repentance." This is the day of salvation, not the day of judgment.

Peter made reference to Paul's writings, because it is Paul, more than any other New Testament writer, who explained God's plan for mankind during this present age. Especially in Romans and Ephesians, Paul explained the relationship between Israel and the church. He pointed out that God used the nation Israel to prepare the way for the coming of the Saviour. But Israel rejected its King and asked to have Him crucified. Did this destroy God's plan? Of course not! Today, Israel is set aside nationally, but God is doing a wonderful new thing: He is saving Jews and Gentiles, and making them one in Christ in the church!

For centuries, if a Gentile wanted to be saved, he had to come by way of Israel. This same attitude persisted even in the early church (Acts 15). Paul made it clear that *both* Jews and Gentiles stand condemned before God and that both must be saved by faith in Jesus Christ. In Jesus Christ, saved Jews and Gentiles belong to the one body, the church. The church is a "mystery" that was hidden in God's counsels and later revealed through the New Testament prophets and apostles (see Eph. 3).

The Jewish nation was God's great testimony to Law, but the church is His witness for grace (see Eph. 1—2). Law prepared the way for grace, and grace enables us to fulfill the righteousness of the Law (Rom. 8:1-5). This does not mean that there was no grace under the Old Covenant, or that New Covenant believers are lawless! Anyone who was saved under the administration of Law was saved by grace, through faith, as Romans 4 and Hebrews 11 make clear.

Now, unlearned and unstable people have a difficult time understanding Paul's teachings. Even some learned and stable people who have spiritual discernment can find themselves floundering in great passages like Romans 9—11! Some Bible students, in their attempt to "harmonize" seeming contradictions (Law and grace, Israel and the church, faith and works) twist the Scriptures and try to make them teach what is really not there. The Greek word translated *wrest* means "to torture on the rack, to distort and pervert."

Even in Paul's day, there were those who twisted his words and tried to defend their ignorance. They accused Paul of teaching that, since we are saved by grace, it makes no difference how we live! It was "slanderously reported" that Paul taught, "Let us do evil that good may come" (Rom. 3:8; cf. Rom. 6:1ff). Others accused Paul of being against the Law because he taught the equality of Jews and Gentiles in the church (Gal. 3:28) and their liberty in Christ.

Most heresies are the perversion of some fundamental doctrine of the Bible. False teachers take verses out of context, twist the Scriptures, and manufacture doctrines that are contrary to the Word of God. Peter probably had the false teachers in mind, but the warning is good for all of us. We must accept the teaching of the Scriptures and not try to make them say what we want them to say.

Note that Peter classified Paul's letters as *Scripture*, that is, the inspired Word of God. Not only did the teaching of the apostles agree with that of the prophets and our Lord (2 Peter 3:2), but the apostles also agreed with each other. Some liberal scholars try to prove that the apostles' doctrine was different from that of Jesus Christ, or that Peter and Paul were at variance with each other. The recipients of Peter's second letter had also read some of Paul's epistles, and Peter assured them that there was agreement.

What happens to people who blindly twist the Scriptures? They do it "unto their own destruction." Peter was not writing about Christians who have a difficult time interpreting the Word of God, because nobody understands *all* of the Bible perfectly. He was describing the false teachers who "tortured" the Word of God in order to prove their false doctrines. I once listened to a cultist "explain" why the group's leader was the "new Messiah" by manipulating the "weeks" in Daniel 9:23-27. He twisted the prophecy unmercifully!

The word *destruction* is repeated often in this letter (2 Peter 2:1-3; 3:7, 16). In the *King James Version*, it is translated "damnable," "pernicious," and "perdition," as well as "destruction." It means the rejection of eternal life, which results in eternal death.

Since this is the day of salvation, we must be diligent to do all we can to win the lost. We do not know how long the Lord will be "long-suffering" toward this evil world. We must not presume on His grace. We must understand what the Bible teaches about God's program for this present age, and we must be motivated by a love for the lost (2 Cor. 5:14) and a desire to be pleasing to Him when He returns.

The false teachers are multiplying and their pernicious doctrines are infecting the church. God needs separated men and women who will resist them, live godly lives, and bear witness of the saving grace of Jesus Christ. The time is short!

Be Diligent to Grow Spiritually (2 Peter 3:17-18)
There are four "beloved" statements in 2 Peter 3 which summarize what Peter wanted to get across as he brought his second letter to a close.

"Beloved . . . be mindful" (3:1-2).
"Beloved, be not ignorant" (3:8).
"Beloved . . . be diligent" (3:14).
"Beloved . . . beware" (3:17).

The word translated *beware* means "be constantly guarding yourself." Peter's readers knew the truth, but he warned them that knowledge alone was not sufficient protection. They had to be on their guard; they had to be alert. It is easy for people who have a knowledge of the Bible to grow over-confident and to forget the warning, "Wherefore let him that thinketh he standeth take heed lest he fall" (1 Cor. 10:12).

What special danger did Peter see? That the true believers would be "led away together with the error of the wicked" (literal translation). He is warning us against breaking down the walls of separation that must stand between the true believers and the false teachers. There can be no communion between truth and error. The apostates "live in error" (2 Peter 2:18), while true believers live in the sphere of the truth (2 John 1-2).

The word *wicked* (2 Peter 3:17) means "the lawless." Peter's description of the apostates in 2 Peter 2 reveals how lawless they are. They even speak evil of the authorities that seek to enforce God's Law in this world! (2:10-11) They promise their converts freedom (2:19), but that freedom turns out to be lawlessness.

True Christians cannot fall from salvation and be lost, but they can fall from their own "steadfastness." What was this steadfastness? Being "established in the present truth" (1:12). The stability of the Christian comes from his faith in

the Word of God, his knowledge of that Word, and his ability to use that Word in the practical decisions of life.

One of the great tragedies of evangelism is bringing "spiritual babies" into the world and then failing to feed them,
nurture them, and help them develop. The apostates prey on
young believers who have "very recently escaped" from the
ways of error (2:18). New believers need to be taught the
basic doctrines of the Word of God; otherwise, they will be
in danger of being "led away with the error of the lawless."

How can we as believers maintain our steadfastness and
avoid being among the "unstable souls" who are easily be-
guiled and led astray? By growing spiritually. "But be constantly growing" is the literal translation. We should not
grow "in spurts," but in a constant experience of development.

We must grow "in grace." This has to do with Christian
character traits, the very things Peter wrote about in 1:5-7,
and that Paul wrote about in Galatians 5:22-23. We were
saved by grace (Eph. 2:8-9), but grace does not end there!
We must also be strengthened by grace (2 Tim. 2:1-4). God's
grace can enable us to endure suffering (2 Cor. 12:7-10). His
grace also helps us to give when giving is difficult (2 Cor.
8:1ff) and to sing when singing is difficult (Col. 3:16).

Our God is "the God of all grace" (1 Peter 5:10), who
"giveth grace unto the humble" (James 4:6). As we study His
Word, we learn about the various aspects of grace that are
available to us as children of God. We are stewards of "the
manifold grace of God" (1 Peter 4:10). There is grace for
every situation and every challenge of life. "But by the grace
of God I am what I am" wrote Paul (1 Cor. 15:10), and that
should be our testimony as well.

Growing in grace often means experiencing trials and even
suffering. We never really experience the grace of God until
we are at the end of our own resources. The lessons learned

in the "school of grace" are always costly lessons, but they are worth it. To grow in grace means to become more like the Lord Jesus Christ, from whom we receive all the grace that we need (John 1:16).

We must also grow in knowledge. How easy it is to grow in knowledge but not in grace! All of us know far more of the Bible than we really live. Knowledge without grace is a terrible weapon, and grace without knowledge can be very shallow. But when we combine grace and knowledge, we have a marvelous tool for building our lives and for building the church.

But note that we are challenged to grow, not just in knowledge of the Bible, as good as that is, but "in the knowledge of our Lord and Saviour Jesus Christ." It is one thing to "know the Bible," and quite another thing to know the Son of God, the central theme of the Bible. The better we know Christ through the Word, the more we grow in grace; the more we grow in grace, the better we understand the Word of God.

So, the separated Christian must constantly be *guarding* himself, lest he be led away into error; he also must be constantly *growing* in grace and knowledge. This requires diligence! It demands discipline and priorities. Nobody automatically drifts into spiritual growth and stability, but anybody can drift *out of* dedication and growth. "For this reason we must pay much closer attention to what we have heard, lest we drift away from it" (Heb. 2:1, NASB). Just as the boat needs the anchor, so the Christian needs the Word of God.

Physical growth and spiritual growth follow pretty much the same pattern. To begin with, we grow from the inside out. "As newborn babes" is the way Peter illustrated it (1 Peter 2:2). The child of God is born with everything he needs for growth and service (2 Peter 1:3). All he needs is the spiritual food and exercise that will enable him to develop. He needs to keep clean. We grow by nutrition, not by addition!

We grow best in a loving family, and this is where the local church comes in. A baby needs a family for protection, provision, and affection. Tests prove that babies who are raised alone, without special love, tend to develop physical and emotional problems very early. The church is God's "nursery" for the care and feeding of Christians, the God-ordained environment that encourages them to grow.

It is important that we grow in a balanced way. The human body grows in a balanced way with the various limbs working together; likewise the "spiritual man" must grow in a balanced way. We must grow in grace and knowledge (3:18), for example. We must keep a balance between worship and service, between faith and works. A balanced diet of the whole Word of God helps us to maintain a balanced life.

It is the Holy Spirit of God who empowers and enables us to keep things in balance. Before Peter was filled with the Spirit, he was repeatedly going to extremes. He would bear witness to Christ one minute and then try to argue with the Lord the next! (Matt. 16:13-23) He refused to allow Jesus to wash his feet, and then he wanted to be washed all over! (John 13:6-10) He promised to defend the Lord and even die with Him, yet he did not have the courage to *own* the Lord before a little servant girl! But when he was filled with the Spirit, Peter began to live a balanced life that avoided impulsive extremes.

What is the result of spiritual growth? Glory to God! "To Him be glory both now and forever." It glorifies Jesus Christ when we keep ourselves separated from sin and error. It glorifies Him when we grow in grace and knowledge, for then we become more like Him (Rom. 8:29). In his life and even in his death, Peter glorified God (John 21:18-19).

As you review this important epistle, you cannot help but be struck by the urgency of the message. The apostates are here! They are busy! They are seducing immature Christians! We must be guarding, growing, and glorifying the Lord, making the most of every opportunity to win the lost and strengthen the saved.

Be diligent! The ministry you save may be your own!

8

A Faithful Family

2 John

The apostate teachers not only invaded the churches, but they also tried to influence Christian homes. Titus faced this problem in Crete (Titus 1:10-11) and Timothy faced it in Ephesus (2 Tim. 3:6). As goes the home, so goes the church and the nation; thus the family is an important target in Satan's war against truth.

This brief letter was written to a godly mother and her children. Some Bible students have concluded that "the elect lady" refers to a local church and that "her children" are the believers fellowshipping in the church. "Thy elect sister" (2 John 13) would then refer to a sister church that was sending Christian greetings.

While it is true that John does address a group in this letter (note the plural in vv. 6, 8, 10, 12), it is also true that he addresses an individual (vv. 1, 4-5, 13). Perhaps the solution is that a Christian assembly was meeting in this home, along with the family of the "elect lady," so that John had both the family and the congregation in mind (see Rom. 16:5; 1 Cor. 16:19; Col. 4:15; Phile. 2). He was concerned that this godly woman not permit anything false to come into her house (2 John 10) or into the assembly.

The dominant feelings in this little epistle are those of friendship and joy, even though these are mixed with concern and warning. If you and I are to keep our homes true to Christ, then we must have the same characteristics as this family to which John wrote.

We Must Know the Truth (2 John 1-3)

John used the word *truth* four times in this salutation, so it is an important word. Basically, it means "reality" as opposed to mere appearance, the *ultimate* that is the basis for all that we see around us. Jesus Christ is "the truth" (John 14:6) and God's Word is "truth" (John 17:17). God has revealed truth in the person of His Son and in the pages of His Word. He has given us "the Spirit of truth" to teach us and to enable us to know truth (John 14:16-17; 16:13).

But the truth is not only an objective revelation from the Father, but also a subjective experience in our personal lives. We cannot only *know* the truth, but we can "love in the truth" and live "for the truth's sake." The truth "lives in us, and shall be with us forever." This means that "knowing the truth" is much more than giving assent to a body of doctrines, though that is important. It means that the believer's life is controlled by a love for the truth and a desire to magnify the truth.

John opened his letter on this note of "truth" because there were false teachers abroad who were spreading error. He called them deceivers and antichrists (2 John 7). John was not one to say that all religious teachings are true in one way or another, and that we should not be critical just as long as people are sincere. To John, there was a great difference, in fact, a deadly difference, between truth and error; and he would not tolerate error.

Since the truth will be with us forever, we certainly ought to get acquainted with it now and learn to love it. Of course, all truth centers in Jesus Christ, the eternal Son of God, with whom we shall live forever (John 14:1-6). It is wonderful to contemplate the fact that we shall spend eternity surrounded by truth, growing in our knowledge of truth, and serving the God of truth.

How did this elect lady and her children come to know the truth and become children of God? Through the grace and mercy of God (2 John 3). God is rich in mercy and grace (Eph. 2:4, 7), and He has channeled His mercy and grace to us in Jesus Christ. We are not saved by God's love, but by God's grace, which is "love that paid a price" (Eph. 2:8-9). God loves the whole world, yet the whole world is not saved. Only those who receive His abundant grace experience salvation from sin.

When you receive grace and mercy from God, you experience His peace. "Therefore, being justified [declared righteous] by faith, we have peace with God through our Lord Jesus Christ"(Rom. 5:1). God is not at war with lost sinners; it is sinners who are at war with God (Rom. 5:10; 8:7). God has been reconciled to sinners because of Christ's work on the cross. Now sinners must repent and be reconciled to God by faith in Jesus Christ (2 Cor. 5:14-21).

It is significant that at the very outset of his second letter John affirmed the deity of Jesus Christ. He did so by joining "the Lord Jesus Christ" with "God the Father." Suppose verse 3 read "from God the Father, and from the Prophet Amos." You would immediately respond, "Amos must not be joined with the Father's name in that fashion! It makes it appear that Amos is equal with God!"

But that is exactly why John joined the Father and the Son together: they are equally God! And then, to make certain that his readers did not miss the emphasis, John added "the

Son of the Father." It is impossible to separate the two. If God is the Father, then He must have a Son; Jesus Christ is that Son. "Whosoever denieth the Son, the same hath not the Father" (1 John 2:23).

Many false teachers argue, "But Jesus is the 'son of God' in the same way all of us are God's sons, made in the image of God! When Jesus claimed to be God's Son, He was not really claiming to be God." But when Jesus said to the Jews, "I and My Father are one," they threatened to stone Him! Why? Because He had blasphemed! "Because that Thou, being a man, makest Thyself God" (John 10:30-33). They knew what He meant when He called Himself the "Son of God" and claimed equality with God.

The Christian faith stands or falls on the doctrine of the deity of Jesus Christ. If He is only man, then He cannot save us, no matter how gifted or unique He might be. If He is not God come in human flesh, then the Christian faith is lies—not truth—and John opened this letter with the wrong emphasis.

The great American statesman Daniel Webster was dining in Boston with a group of distinguished men, some of whom had Unitarian leanings. (The Unitarians deny the Trinity and the deity of both the Son and the Spirit.) When the subject of religion came up at the table, Webster boldly affirmed his belief in the deity of Jesus Christ and his confidence in His work of atonement.

"But Mr. Webster," said one man, "can you comprehend how Christ could be both God and man?"

"No, sir, I cannot comprehend it," Webster replied. "If I could comprehend Him, He would be no greater than myself. I feel that I need a superhuman Saviour!"

If our homes and churches are to be true to Christ and oppose the false teachers, we must know the truth. How do we learn the truth? By carefully studying God's Word and allowing the Spirit to teach us; by listening to others who are true to the faith; and then by practicing what we learn. We must not only *learn* the truth with our minds, but we must also *love* the truth in our hearts and *live* the truth by our wills. Our total persons must be yielded to the truth.

How important it is for parents to teach their children to love the truth! While we thank God for Sunday Schools and Christian day schools, in the final analysis, it is the home that must instill in children a love for truth and the knowledge of God's truth.

We Must Walk in the Truth (2 John 4-6)

To "walk in the truth" means to obey it, to permit it to control every area of our lives. This paragraph opens and closes with an emphasis on obedience, walking in the truth. It is much easier to study the truth, or even argue about the truth, than it is to practice it! In fact, sometimes zealous Christians disobey the truth in the very way they try to defend it.

When I was pastoring in Chicago, a strange young man often stood on the sidewalk in front of the church, passing out leaflets that denounced many evangelical leaders who were my friends. Of course, we could not stop him from distributing literature, so I instructed our people to take as many copies as he would give them and then destroy them!

One of our men decided to "shadow" the young man one evening, and he saw him walk to the nearby park, sit down under a tree, and light up a cigarette! Yet just a few minutes before, the young man had been shouting in front of the church, "I'm a fighting fundamentalist, and I'm not ashamed of it!" My guess is that most of the fundamentalists I know would have been ashamed of him. He thought he was promoting truth and opposing error, yet he was not walking in the truth himself. By his actions and belligerent attitude, he was denying the truth he sought to defend.

THE APOSTLE'S JOY (v. 4a) was that the elect lady's children were walking in truth. John did not know all of them, however; the literal translation is "some of thy children." Somewhere in his travels, John had met some of her children and learned of their obedient walk with the Lord. "I have no greater joy than to hear that my children walk in truth" (3 John 4). We have no reason to believe that John was hinting that others of the children had gone astray after the false teachers. If by "children" John was including the members of the "house church," then it is possible that some of them had left the fellowship and joined with the deceivers.

It certainly brings great joy to the Father when He sees His children obeying His Word. I know personally what it means to the pastor when the church family is submissive to the Word and doing the will of God. Few things break the heart of a pastor like a disobedient and rebellious member who will not submit to the authority of God's Word.

When the great Baptist preacher Charles Spurgeon was a lad, he lived with his grandfather who pastored a church in Stambourne, England. A church member named Roads used to sit in the local pub and drink beer and smoke, and this practice grieved the pastor very much.

One day young Charles said to his grandfather, "I'll kill old Roads, that I will! I shall not do anything bad, but I'll kill him though, that I will!"

What did young Spurgeon do? He confronted Roads in the pub with these words: "What doest thou here, Elijah? Sitting with the ungodly, and you a member of a church and breaking your pastor's heart. I'm ashamed of you! I wouldn't break my pastor's heart, I'm sure!"

It was not long before Roads showed up at the pastor's home, confessing his sins and apologizing for his behavior. Young Spurgeon had "killed him" indeed!

THE APOSTLE'S ARGUMENT (v. 4b) is that God has commanded us to walk in truth and love. The word *commandment* is
used five times in these few verses. God's commandments
focus "the truth" on specific areas of life. "The truth" can be
vague and general if we are not careful, but "the commandments" make that truth specific and binding.

Note that the commandments are given by "the Father."
Each commandment is an expression of love and not simply
law. The will of God is the revelation of God's heart (Ps.
33:11), not just His mind. Consequently, obedience to His
Word should be a revelation of *our* love, not an expression of
fear. "For this is the love of God, that we keep His commandments: and His commandments are not grievous"
(1 John 5:3).

The false teachers try to make God's commandments appear harsh and difficult and then they offer their converts
"true" freedom (2 Peter 2:19). But the greatest freedom is in
obedience to God's perfect will. No believer who loves God
would ever consider His commandments to be harsh and
unbearable.

THE APOSTLE'S APPEAL (vv. 5-6) is that the elect lady and her
family love one another and this appeal applies to us as well.
"A new commandment I give unto you, 'That ye love one
another' " (John 13:34). But John wrote that it was *not* a
new commandment (see 1 John 2:7-11). Is this a contradiction?

The commandment "Love one another" is certainly not
new in time, because even Old Testament Jews were instructed to love their neighbors (Lev. 19:18, 34) and the
strangers within their gates (Deut. 10:19). But with the coming of God's Son to earth, this commandment is new in
emphasis and in example. Jesus Christ gave new emphasis to
brotherly love, and He exemplified it in His own life. It is
also new in experience, for we have the Holy Spirit of God

living within, enabling us to obey. "But the fruit of the Spirit is love" (Gal. 5:22; cf. Rom. 5:5).

Is it possible to *command* love? Yes, when you understand what Christian love really is. Many people have the mistaken idea that Christian love is a feeling, a special kind of "religious emotion" that makes us reach out and accept others. Certainly emotion is involved, but basically, Christian love is *an act of the will.* It simply means treating other people the same way God treats you! In fact, it is possible to love people that we really do not "like."

We may not be able to will our affections at all times, but we can will our attitudes and actions. When people are rude to us, we can be kind in return. When people persecute us, we can pray for them and, when the opportunity comes, do good to them. If we followed our feelings, we would probably retaliate! But if we ask the Spirit to control our wills, then we can act toward them, as Jesus would have acted, in Christian love.

John went on to explain that love and obedience must go together (2 John 6). It is impossible to divorce our relationship with God from our relationship with people. If we say that we love God, but we hate our brother, then we can be sure that we do not really love God (1 John 4:20). If we obey God, then His love is perfected in us, and we have no problem loving our brother (1 John 2:3-5).

As you review this paragraph, you note three themes that blend: truth, love, and obedience. It is by believing the truth—in Christ and in the Word—that we are saved. The evidence of that salvation is love and obedience, but love and obedience are strengthened as we grow in our knowledge of truth. We speak the truth in love (Eph. 4:15) and we obey God's commandments because we love Him. Obedience enables us to learn more truth (John 7:17), and the more truth we learn, the more we love Jesus Christ who is truth!

Instead of living in a "vicious circle," we live in a "victorious circle" of love, truth, and obedience!

We Must Abide in the Truth (2 John 7-11)

From encouraging truth, John turned to opposing error. He joined his voice with Peter's to warn that there are deceivers in the world. The word *deceiver* implies much more than teaching false doctrine. It also includes leading people into wrong living. John has already made it clear that *truth and life go together.* What we believe determines how we behave. Wrong doctrine and wrong living always go together.

Where did these false teachers come from originally? "For many deceivers have gone out into the world" (literal translation). They went out *from the church!* At one time, they professed to believe "the faith which was once delivered unto the saints" (Jude 3), but they turned from that faith and abandoned the truth and the church. "They went out from us, but they were not of us" (1 John 2:19). "Also of your own selves shall men arise, speaking perverse things, to draw away disciples after them" (Acts 20:30).

It takes constant spiritual vigilance to protect a family or a local church from the insidious attacks of false teachers. One very successful pastor told me, "If I took my eyes off this work for twenty-four hours and stopped praying, it would be invaded before we knew it." He was not emphasizing his own importance (though godly pastors are essential to spiritual churches) but the importance of diligence and vigilance.

Note that there are *many* deceivers! Why? Second Peter 2:2 gives the answer: "And many shall follow their pernicious ways." I think it was Mark Twain who said that a lie runs around the world while truth is putting on her shoes. Fallen human nature wants to believe lies and resist God's truth. We have already learned from 2 Peter 2 the devious methods the apostates use to seduce unwary and unstable people. No wonder they are successful!

These deceivers are also "antichrists" (see 1 John 2:18-29). The Greek prefix *anti* means both "instead of" and "against." These teachers are *against* Christ because they deny that He is indeed God come in the flesh (see 1 John 4:1-6). They not only deny the truth about Christ, but they give their converts a "substitute Christ" who is not the Christ of the Christian faith. The first question you want to ask any teacher, preacher, or author is, "What do you think about Christ? Is He God come in the flesh?" If he hesitates, or if he denies that Jesus is God come in the flesh, then you can be sure you have a false teacher.

I was preaching at Carrubers Close Mission in Edinburgh, Scotland, and before the meeting started, a young man came up to me. Without even introducing himself, he said, "Do you believe in the virgin birth of Jesus Christ?" I replied emphatically that I did, and that I preached that Jesus Christ was the Son of God come in the flesh. While I did not appreciate his arrogant manner, I did appreciate his concern that the man in the pulpit was "abiding in the truth."

To *abide in the truth* means to remain true to the basic doctrines of the Christian faith. The false teachers had departed from the truth and from the church fellowship and, therefore, they were dangerous. John pointed out three dangers the church and its members face because of deceivers in the world.

THE DANGER OF GOING BACK (v. 8). This is the danger of losing what has already been gained. *Look to yourselves* means "Beware! Take heed!" The false teachers offer something you do not have, when in reality they take away what you already have!

Satan is a thief and so are his helpers. John wanted his readers to receive "a full reward," which is his equivalent of 2 Peter 1:11, an abundant entrance into the eternal kingdom. What a tragedy it is when God's servants labor faithfully to build up a church, and then the work is destroyed by false teaching. No wonder Paul wrote to the Galatian assemblies, "I am afraid of [for] you, lest I have bestowed upon you labor in vain" (Gal. 4:11).

"Do not lose the things we accomplished" is the way Kenneth Wuest translates verse 8. Church members need to respect the work of faithful pastors and teachers and do everything to protect it and extend it. God's servants must one day give an account of their ministries, and they want to do it "with joy and not with grief" (Heb. 13:17). When the church goes backward, losing what it has gained, then it also will lose part of the reward at the Judgment Seat of Christ. It is essential that we hold fast to the truth of the Word of God!

THE DANGER OF GOING AHEAD (v. 9). The danger here is that of going beyond the limits of the Word of God and adding to it. The word translated *transgress* means "to run ahead too far, to pass beyond the assigned limits." It is false progress! The apostates like to make us believe that they are "progressive" while the church is "in a rut." They invite us to join them because they have something "new and exciting" to share. But their "progress" is such that they abandon the doctrine that Jesus Christ is the Son of God come in the flesh.

Fifty years ago, the American press was filled with news about "the fundamentalist-modernist controversy." Those who were true to the faith were opposing "modernism" in the mainline denominations and seeking to bring the schools and the leadership of these denominations back to historic Christianity. The "progressive" group called themselves "modernists," when actually there was nothing "modern" about their denials of Christian doctrine. These denials are as old as the church itself! One of their leaders, Dr. Harry Emerson Fosdick, said in one of his sermons, "Fundamentalism is still with us but mostly in the backwaters." If he were alive today, he would not make that statement; today the largest Sunday Schools, churches, seminaries, and missionary agencies are fundamental in doctrine.

If a person does not abide in the true doctrine, then he does not have either the Father or the Son. It is impossible to honor the Father and ignore the Son (or call Him a mere man) at the same time. "That all men should honor the Son, even as they honor the Father. He that honoreth not the Son honoreth not the Father which hath sent Him" (John 5:23). "Progressive theology" that denies Christ is not progressive at all; it is regressive—all the way back to Genesis 3:1, "Yea, hath God said?"

In giving this warning, however, John was not condemning "progress" as such. "The Lord has yet more light to shine forth from His Word." God gave us the Holy Spirit to teach us and to lead us into new understanding and application of the truth (John 16:12-16), and we must constantly grow (2 Peter 3:18).

But if our "learning" leads us away from the fundamental doctrines of the person and work of Jesus Christ, then we are on dangerous ground.

THE DANGER OF GOING WITH (vv. 10-11). John warned the family (and the church in their house) not to accept false teachers who visited them, wanting to fellowship with them or perhaps enjoy hospitality. Hospitality was a very important Christian ministry in that day, because there were very few inns where travelers could safely stay, especially Christians who wanted to keep away from the evil influences of the world. Christians were admonished to open their homes to visitors (Rom. 12:13; 1 Tim. 3:2; 5:3-10; Heb. 13:2; 1 Peter 4:8-10).

It was also true that traveling pastors and teachers needed homes to stay in (3 John 5-8). Believers who showed hospitality to these servants of God were "fellowhelpers to the truth," but believers who assisted false teachers were only sharing in their evil works. The doctrine of Jesus Christ is a test of truth, a basis for fellowship, and a bond for mutual cooperation.

Certainly this principle applies today. Often professed Christians come to our doors, wanting to play cassettes for us or offering us magazines or books. We must exercise discernment. If they do not agree with the true doctrine of Christ, not only must we not let them in, but we must not even say "good-bye," which means "God be with you."

Why was John so adamant about this? Because he did not want any of God's children to: (1) give a false teacher the impression that his heretical doctrine was acceptable; (2) become infected because of association and possible friendship; and (3) give the false teacher ammunition to use at the next place he stopped. If I entertain a cultist, for example, he will only say to the neighbors, "There's no reason why you shouldn't let me in. After all, Pastor Wiersbe let me in and we had a wonderful talk!" My disobedience could very well lead to somebody else's destruction.

Let me make it clear that John was not saying only born-again people should enter our houses! "Friendship evangelism" around the table is a wonderful way to win people to Christ. Christians needs to be neighborly and hospitable. The apostle is admonishing us not to receive or encourage *false teachers who represent antichristian groups*, people who have left the church and are now trying to seduce others away from the truth. You can be sure that apostates use every opportunity they can to secure the endorsement of true Christians.

There is a tradition about the Apostle John that illustrates his position concerning false doctrine. When he was living in Ephesus, one day he went to the public baths, and there he saw Cerinthus, the leader of a heretical sect. John ran from the buildings lest they should fall down as a judgment from God! Cerinthus taught that Jesus was the natural son of Joseph and Mary, not God come in the flesh.

John's closing words (2 John 12-13) are almost identical to the farewell in 3 John, and they require no explanation. They do, however, express the importance of Christian fellowship and the joy that it should bring to our hearts (see 1 John 1:4). It is wonderful to receive letters, but even more wonderful to receive God's people into our homes and hearts.

This little epistle, written to a Christian mother and her family (and perhaps the church in their house), is a perfect gem of sacred correspondence. But we must not forget the major thrust of the letter: be alert! There are many deceivers in the world!

9

It's the Truth

3 John

The battle for truth and against apostasy is fought not only in the home (2 John) but especially in the local church; and that is where 3 John comes in. This little letter (the shortest New Testament epistle in the original Greek) gives us a glimpse into an early assembly, its people, and its problems. As you read this brief letter, you find yourself saying, "Times have not changed very much!" We have similar people and problems today!

One of the key words in this letter is *witness* (v. 3, "testified"; v. 6; v. 12, "report, bear record, record"). It means not only the words that we say but the lives that we live. Each Christian is a witness, either a good one or a bad one. We are either helping the truth (v. 8) or hindering it.

This letter was addressed to Gaius, one of the leaders of the assembly. But John also discussed two other men in these verses—Diotrephes and Demetrius. Wherever there are people, there are problems—and the potential for *solving* problems. Each of us must honestly face the question, "Am I a part of the problem or a part of the answer?"

Consider the three men involved in this letter and note the kinds of Christians they were.

Gaius the Encourager (3 John 1-8)

There is no question that the Apostle John dearly loved this man! He called him "the well beloved" in his greeting, and "beloved" in verse 5. It is unlikely that these were merely formal terms, like our "Dear Mr. Jones." (We may not even know Mr. Jones personally!) Verse 4 suggests that Gaius may have been one of John's converts, and, of course, those we lead to faith in Christ are especially precious to us. However, the beloved apostle looked on all the believers as his "little children" (1 John 2:1, 12, 18), so we must not press this too far.

If Gaius were a member of a church that I pastored, I would certainly have no trouble loving him! Consider the personal qualities of this excellent man.

SPIRITUAL HEALTH (v. 2). John may be hinting here that his dear friend was not well and that John was praying for restored health: "I want you to be as healthy in body as you are in soul!" If this is the case, then it is evidence that it is possible to be spiritually healthy and physically sick. However, this kind of a greeting was very common in that day, so we must not build too much on it.

However, it is clear that Gaius was a man whose "spiritual health" was evident to all. "Though our outward man perish, yet the inward man is renewed day by day" (2 Cor. 4:16). Physical health is the result of nutrition, exercise, cleanliness, proper rest, and the disciplined order of a balanced life. Spiritual health is the result of similar factors. We must nourish ourselves with the Word, and then "work out" that nourishment in godly exercise (1 Tim. 4:6-7). We must keep ourselves clean (2 Cor. 7:1) and avoid the contamination and pollution that is in the world (2 Peter 1:4; James

1:27). While exercise and service are important, it is also important that we rest in the Lord and gain new strength through fellowship with Him (Matt. 11:18-30). A balanced life is a healthy and happy life, a life that honors God.

A GOOD TESTIMONY (vv. 3-4). Gaius was recognized as a man who obeyed the Word of God and "walked in truth." (See 2 John 4.) Some of the brethren had made several visits to John, and they had joyfully reported that Gaius was a glowing example of what a Christian ought to be. In my own pastoral experience, I must confess that I have often been a bit "on edge" when people have said to me, "Is Mrs. —— a member of your church?" Or, even worse, "I know one of your members quite well!" John never had to fear when Gaius' name came up!

What made Gaius such a good testimony? *God's truth.* The truth was "in him" and enabled him to walk in obedience to God's will. Gaius read the Word, meditated on it, delighted in it, and then practiced it in his daily life (see Ps. l:1-3). What digestion is to the body, meditation is to the soul. It is not enough merely to *hear* the Word or *read* the Word. We must inwardly "digest it" and make it part of our inner persons (see 1 Thes. 2:13).

It is clear that Gaius' entire life was wrapped up in the truth. True living comes from the living truth. Jesus Christ, the truth (John 14:6), is revealed in the Word, which is God's truth (John 17:17). The Holy Spirit is also truth (1 John 5:7), and He teaches us the truth. The Spirit of God uses the Word of God to reveal the Son of God, and then to enable us to obey the will of God and "walk in truth."

PRACTICAL MINISTRY (vv. 4-8). Gaius was also a fellowhelper to the truth (v. 8). In practical ways, he assisted those who were ministering the Word. We have no indication that Gaius himself was a preacher or teacher, but he opened his heart and home to those who were.

We have learned from John's second letter the importance of Christian hospitality in that day. John warned "the elect lady" against entertaining false teachers (2 John 7-11), but in this letter he commended Gaius for showing hospitality to the true ministers of the Word. Gaius was an encouragement, not only to the brethren in general, but especially to "strangers" who came to fellowship with the church and to minister (see Heb. 13:2).

In this day of fear and violence, it is not easy to welcome strangers into our homes. Of course, in the early church, traveling ministers carried letters of recommendation from their own assembly (Rom. 16:1); so it is important that we know something about the people we plan to entertain. However, it does take faith and love. As much as my wife and I enjoy sharing our home, we must confess that there have been times when bidding our guests good-bye brought a sense of happy relief! For the most part, however, our guests have truly been "angels unawares" whose presence was a blessing in our home.

Gaius not only opened his home, but he also opened his heart and his hand to give financial help to his guests. The phrase *bring forward on their journey* means "to assist on their journey." This could have included providing money and food as well as washing and mending clothing (see 1 Cor. 16:6; Titus 3:13). After all, our faith must be proved by our works (James 2:14-16), and our love must be expressed by deeds, not just words (1 John 3:16-18).

What is the motivation for this kind of practical ministry to the saints? First of all, *it honors God*. The phrase *after a godly sort* in verse 6 means "worthy of God, as befits God." We are never more "Godlike" than when we are sacrificing to serve others. "That ye might walk worthy of the Lord unto all pleasing" (Col. 1:10). Since these itinerant ministers were representing the name of the Lord, any ministry to them was really a service to Jesus Christ (Matt. 10:40; 25:34-40).

A second motive is that the support of God's servants is *a witness to the lost* (3 John 7). Keep in mind that there were many wandering teachers in that day, sharing their ideas and begging for money. While the Lord Jesus taught definitely that God's servants deserve support (Luke 10:7), the standard in the New Testament is that this support comes from God's people. "Taking nothing of the Gentiles" means that these itinerant workers would not solicit help from the unsaved. Abraham had this same policy (Gen. 14:21-24), though he did not force his associates to adopt his policy. Many pastors make it clear, when the offering is being received, that they are not asking anything from the unbelievers in the congregation.

When God's people adequately support God's servants, it is a powerful testimony to the lost. But when ministers, churches, and other religious organizations go about *soliciting* from unsaved people and various businesses, it makes Christianity look cheap and commercial. This does not mean that God's servants should refuse a *voluntary* gift from an unconverted person, as long as the person understands that the gift will not purchase salvation. Even then, we must be very cautious. The king of Sodom's offer was voluntary, but Abraham rejected it! (Gen. 14:17-24)

The third motivation for serving is *obedience to God*. "We therefore ought to receive such" (3 John 8a). This ministry of hospitality and support is not only an opportunity, but also an obligation. Galatians 6:6-10 makes it clear that those who receive *spiritual* blessings from the minister of the Word ought to share with him in *material* blessings; 1 Corinthians 9:7-11 further explains this principle. As a deacon expressed it to me in the first church I pastored, "You pay your board where you get your food!" It is unbiblical for church members to send their tithes and offerings all over the world and neglect to support the ministry of their own local church.

John gave a fourth motivation in verse 8: "That we might be fellowhelpers to the truth." Gaius not only received the truth and walked in the truth, but he was a "jointworker" who helped to further the truth. We do not know what his spiritual gifts were or how he served in the congregation, but we do know that Gaius helped extend and defend the truth by assisting those who taught and preached it.

In my itinerant ministry, I have stayed in many homes and been encouraged in my work. The host and hostess may not have been especially gifted people, but their ministry of gracious hospitality enabled me to exercise my gifts in the church. Whatever blessings came in the ministry will certainly be credited to their accounts! (Phil. 4:17)

It is one thing to fight apostasy and refuse to entertain false teachers, but quite another thing to open our homes (and wallets) to *promote the truth*. We need both the negative and the positive. We need more people like Gaius who are spiritually healthy, obedient to the Word, and sharing what they have for the furtherance of the truth. But, alas, not everybody is a Gaius! We turn now to an entirely different kind of Christian.

Diotrephes the Dictator (3 John 9-10)

It seems like many churches have members who insist on "being boss" and having their own way. I must confess that sometimes it is the pastor who assumes dictatorial powers and forgets that the word *minister* means "a servant." But sometimes it is an officer, perhaps a longtime member of the church who thinks he has "seniority rights."

Our Lord's disciples often argued over which of them would be the greatest in the kingdom (Matt. 18:1ff). Jesus had to remind them that their model for ministry was not the Roman official who "lorded it over" people, but the Saviour Himself who came as a humble servant (Phil. 2:1ff). During more than thirty years of ministry, I have seen the model for ministry change, and the church is suffering because of it. It appears that the "successful minister" today is more like a Madison Avenue tycoon than a submissive servant. In his hand, he holds a wireless telephone, not a towel; in his heart is selfish ambition, not a love for lost souls and for God's sheep.

Diotrephes was motivated by pride. Instead of giving the preeminence to Jesus Christ (Col. 1:18), he claimed it for himself. He had the final say-so about everything in the church, and his decisions were determined by one thing: "What will this do for Diotrephes?" He was most unlike John the Baptist who said, "He [Jesus Christ] must increase, but I must decrease" (John 3:30). The Greek verb indicates that it was the *constant attitude* of Diotrephes to promote himself.

Whenever a church has a resident dictator in its membership there are bound to be problems, because people who are spiritually minded will not tolerate that kind of leadership. The Holy Spirit is grieved when the members of the body are not permitted to exercise their gifts because one member must have his own way. At the Judgment Seat of Christ, we will discover how many hearts have been broken and churches destroyed because of the arrogant "ministries" of people like Diotrephes. Consider what this man was doing.

HE WOULD NOT RECEIVE JOHN (v. 9). It is incredible to think that a church leader (Diotrephes may have been an elder) would not have fellowship with one of our Lord's own apostles! How much Diotrephes could have learned from John! But Jesus Christ was not preeminent in his life, therefore Diotrephes could afford to treat the aged apostle this way.

Why did Diotrephes reject John? The obvious reason seems to be that John challenged the man's right to be dictator in the church. John was a threat to Diotrephes, because John had the authority of an apostle. John knew the truth about Diotrephes and was willing to make it known. Satan was at work in the church because Diotrephes was operating on the basis of pride and self-glorification, two of the devil's chief tools. If John appeared on the scene, Satan would be the loser.

HE LIED ABOUT JOHN (v. 10). The phrase *prating against us with malicious words* means "bringing false and empty charges against us." What Diotrephes was saying about John was sheer nonsense, but there are people who love to hear such talk and who will believe it! Apparently, Diotrephes had made these accusations against John at one of the church meetings when John was not present to defend himself. But John warned that the day would soon come when he would settle accounts with Diotrephes the dictator.

Christians must be careful not to believe everything that they read or hear about God's servants, particularly those servants who have a wide ministry and are well known. I have quit reading certain publications because all they print is undocumented accusations about people whose ministries God is blessing in a singular way. I mentioned a certain publication to a friend of mine one day, and he said, "Yes, I know the editor quite well. He's like a blotter: he takes everything in *and gets it backward!*" We would all do well to filter these reports through Philippians 4:8.

HE REJECTED JOHN'S ASSOCIATES (v. 10). Diotrephes would not even receive the other brethren because they were in fellowship with John! It was "guilt by association." It is impossible to practice this kind of "separation" with any degree of consistency, because nobody can always know all that he needs to know about what his brother is doing! If I refuse to fellowship with you because you have fellowshipped with somebody I disapprove of, how do I know the extent of your fellowship? How can I keep track of what you have done? A person would need a computer and a full-time staff if he ever hoped to do a good job of keeping his associations pure!

Scripture makes it clear that we should have no fellowship with apostates (we studied this in 2 Peter), and that we must refrain from entangling alliances with unbelievers (2 Cor. 6:14ff). We must also avoid those whose doctrinal position is contrary to Scripture (Rom. 16:17-19). This does not mean that we cooperate only with those believers who interpret Scripture exactly as we do, because even good and godly people disagree on some matters such as church government or prophecy. All true Christians can agree on the fundamental doctrines of the faith and, in love, give latitude for disagreement on other matters.

However, to break personal fellowship with a brother because I disagree with his circle of friends is, to me, going beyond Scripture. Diotrephes rejected John, and then rejected the believers associated with John! But he went even further. HE DISCIPLINED THOSE WHO DISAGREED WITH HIM (v. 10). The church members who received John's associates were dismissed from the church! Again, it was guilt by association. Diotrephes had neither the authority nor the biblical basis for throwing these people out of the church, but he did it. Even "religious dictators" have to be careful lest the opposition become too strong!

The New Testament does teach church discipline, and these instructions ought to be obeyed. But church discipline is not a weapon for a dictator to use to protect himself. It is a tool for a congregation to use to promote purity and glorify God. It is not a pastor "throwing weight around," or a church board acting like a police court. It is the Lord exercising spiritual authority through a local church in order to rescue and restore an erring child of God.

Church "dictators" are dangerous people but, fortunately, they are easy to recognize. They like to talk about themselves and what they have "done for the Lord." They also have the habit of judging and condemning those who disagree with them. They are experts in putting labels on other Christians and classifying them into neat little categories of their own intention. They base their fellowship on personalities, not the doctrines that are fundamental to the faith. The tragedy is that these "dictators" actually believe that they are serving God and glorifying Jesus Christ.

It has been my experience that most of the distress and division in local churches, and between churches, has result- ed from personalities more than anything else. If only we would return to the New Testament principle of making the person and work of Jesus Christ our test for fellowship, rath- er than associations and interpretations of nonessential doc- trines. But people like Diotrephes will always have their en- thusiastic followers because many sincere but immature and untaught believers prefer to follow men.

Demetrius the Exemplar (3 John 11-12)

According to the dictionary, an *exemplar* is "an ideal, a model, an example worthy to be imitated." Demetrius was that kind of a Christian. John warned his readers not to imitate Diotrephes. "If you want to imitate an example, then follow Demetrius!"

But is it right for us to imitate human leaders? Yes, if they in turn are imitating Jesus Christ. "Brethren, be followers together of me, and mark them which walk so as ye have us for an example" (Phil. 3:17). "Be ye followers of me, even as I also am of Christ" (1 Cor. 11:1). You and I cannot see God, but we can see God at work in the lives of His children. The godly life and dedicated service of another believer is always an encouragement and a stimulus to me. By our good example, we can "consider one another to provoke unto love and to good works" (Heb. 10:24).

Demetrius was a man worth imitating because he had a "good report" (witness) from the church fellowship. All the members knew him, loved him, and thanked God for his consistent life and ministry. While it is a dangerous thing when "all men shall speak well of you" (Luke 6:26), it is a wonderful thing when all the believers in a local church can agree to commend your life and testimony. If all men, saved and lost, good and evil, speak well of us, it may mean that we are compromising and masquerading.

But Demetrius not only had a good witness from the believers in the church, he also had a good witness from the Word (truth) itself. Like Gaius, Demetrius walked in the truth and obeyed the Word of God. This does not mean that either of these men was perfect, but it does mean that they were consistent in their lives, seeking to honor the Lord.

Both the church and the Word bore witness to Demetrius' Christian life, and so did the Apostle John himself. (This meant that Demetrius would be in trouble with Diotrephes!) The beloved apostle knew firsthand that Demetrius was a man of God, and John was not ashamed to confess it.

John had warned that he was going to visit the church and confront Diotrephes (3 John 10), and no doubt both Gaius and Demetrius would stand with John in opposing the "dictator." They were the kind of men who would support the truth and submit themselves to authentic spiritual authority. Because they followed the truth, they could safely be imitated by other believers.

The conclusion of the letter (vv. 13-14) is similar to the conclusion of 2 John, and perhaps was a standard way to end letters in John's day. The apostle planned to visit the church "shortly" (soon), which certainly was a warning to

Diotrephes and an encouragement to Gaius and Demetrius. The beloved John had "many things" to discuss with the assembly and its leaders, things he would rather deal with personally rather than by means of a letter.

"Peace be to thee" (v. 14) must have been a benediction of real encouragement to Gaius! No doubt his own heart and mind were distressed because of the division in the church and the unspiritual way Diotrephes was abusing its members. George Morrison of Glasgow wrote, "Peace is the possession of adequate resources." The believer can enjoy the "peace of God" because he has adequate resources in Jesus Christ (Phil. 4:6-7, 13, 19).

John was careful to send greetings from the believers in the assembly with which he was associated at that time. "The friends send their greeting!" (NIV) What a blessing it is to have Christian friends! When Paul arrived near Rome, some of the brethren went to meet him, "whom when Paul saw, he thanked God and took courage" (Acts 28:15). Both Paul and John were not only soul-winners, but also friend-makers. Diotrephes was so dictatorial that he had fewer and fewer friends, but John had more and more friends as he shared the love of Christ.

"Greet the friends by name" (NASB). The aged apostle did not want to write a long letter; besides, he was planning a visit. Paul sometimes ended his letters with a list of personal greetings (see Rom. 16), but John did not do this, at least in this letter. He wanted to have Gaius convey his greetings to his friends personally and individually, as though John were doing it himself. John was not concerned about a church only, but also the individuals within that church.

It is interesting to contrast these two little letters and to see the balance of truth that John presented. Second John was written to a godly woman about her family, while 3 John was written to a godly man about his church. John warned "the elect lady" about false teachers from the out-side, but he warned Gaius about dictatorial leaders inside the fellowship. The false teachers in 2 John would appeal to *love* so that they might deny *truth*, while Diotrephes would appeal to *truth* as, in a most unloving way, he would attack the brethren.

How important it is to walk "in truth and love" (2 John 3) and hold the truth in love! (Eph. 4:15) To claim to love the truth and yet hate the brethren is to confess ignorance of what the Christian life is all about.

When God's people love Him, the truth, and one another, then the Spirit of God can work in that assembly to glorify Jesus Christ. But when any member of that assembly, includ-ing the pastor, becomes proud and tries to have "the preemi-nence," then the Spirit is grieved and He cannot bless. The church may *outwardly* appear successful, but inwardly it will lack the true unity of the Spirit that makes for a healthy fellowship.

What we need are more people like Gaius and Deme-trius—and fewer like Diotrephes!

10

A Call to Arms!

Jude 1-7

Since the author of this epistle was the brother of James, this would make him the half brother of our Lord Jesus Christ (see Mark 6:3). Our Lord's brothers in the flesh did not believe in Him while He was ministering (John 7:5). But after the Resurrection, James was converted (see 1 Cor. 15:7), and we have every reason to believe that Jude was also saved at that time. Acts 1:14 informs us that "His brethren" were part of the praying group that was awaiting the Holy Spirit; 1 Corinthians 9:5 states that "the brethren of the Lord" were known in the early church.

So much for the identification of the author. Why did Jude write this letter? To warn his readers that the apostates were already on the scene! Peter had prophesied that they would come (2 Peter 2:1-3; 3:3ff), and his prophecy had been fulfilled. Apparently Jude wrote to the same believers who had received Peter's letters, intending to stir them up and remind them to take Peter's warnings to heart. You will discover a number of parallels between Jude and 2 Peter as you study this fascinating but neglected letter.

He wrote to "exhort" them (Jude 3). In the Greek language, this word was used to describe a general giving orders to the army; hence the atmosphere of this letter is "military." Jude had started to write a quiet devotional letter about salvation, but the Spirit led him to put down his harp and sound the trumpet! The Epistle of Jude is a call to arms.

The Army (Jude 1-2)

The captain of the army is Jesus Christ, and the soldiers He commands are people who share a "common salvation" through faith in Him. Jude called them *saints* (v. 3), which simply means "set-apart ones." He addressed them as *sanctified*, which, again, means "set apart." (Some manuscripts read "beloved in God the Father.") Perhaps there is an echo here of 1 Peter 1:2 where all three Persons of the Godhead are seen to be involved in our salvation.

Certainly salvation begins in the heart of God and not in the will of man (Rom. 9:16). The mysteries of God's sovereign electing grace are beyond us in this life and will never be understood until we enter His glorious presence. For that reason, we are wise not to make them the basis for arguments and divisions. "The secret things belong unto the Lord our God" (Deut. 29:29).

Second Thessalonians 2:13-14 makes it clear that the same God who chose us also set us apart by the Spirit and then called us by the Gospel to trust in Jesus Christ. God's choosing and God's calling go together, for the God who ordains the end (our salvation) also ordains the *means to the end* (someone calling us to Christ). We did not understand how God's Spirit was working in our lives prior to our conversion, but He was working just the same to "set us apart" for Jesus Christ.

Not only are God's saints set apart, but they are also *preserved*. This means "carefully watched and guarded." The believer is secure in Jesus Christ. This same word is used in Jude 6 and 13 ("reserved") and also in 21 ("keep yourselves"). God is preserving the fallen angels and the apostates for judgment, but He is preserving His own children for glory. Meanwhile, He is able to preserve us in our daily walk and keep us from stumbling.

Because they are set apart and preserved, God's soldiers are the recipients of God's choicest blessings: mercy, peace, and love. Like the Apostle Peter, Jude wanted these special blessings to be *multiplied* in their lives (1 Peter 1:2; 2 Peter 1:2). God in His mercy does not give us what we deserve. Instead, He gave our punishment to His own Son on the cross. "Surely He hath borne our griefs, and carried our sorrows. . . . But He was wounded for our transgressions, He was bruised for our iniquities " (Isa. 53:4-5).

Because of Christ's work on the cross, believers enjoy *peace.* The unsaved person is at war with God and cannot please Him (Rom. 8:7-8); but when he trusts the Saviour, the war ends and he receives God's peace (Rom. 5:1).

He also experiences God's *love* (Rom. 5:5). The Cross is God's demonstration of love (Rom. 5:8), but His love is not experienced within until His Spirit comes into the believing heart. As the believer grows in his spiritual life, he enters into a deeper relationship of love (John 14:21-24).

Certainly those who know Christ as their Saviour enjoy a unique position. They are called *by* God to be set apart *for* God that they might enjoy love *with* God. While their fellowship with the Father might change from day to day, their relationship as children cannot change. They are "preserved in Jesus Christ." Because Jude would write a great deal in this letter about sin and judgment, he was careful at the very outset to define the special place that believers have in the heart and plan of God. The apostates would sin, fall, and suffer condemnation; but the true believers would be kept safe in Jesus Christ for all eternity.

It bears repeating that an apostate is not a true believer who has abandoned his salvation. He is a person who has professed to accept the truth and trust the Saviour, and then turns from "the faith which was once delivered unto the saints" (Jude 3). Jude would not contradict what Peter wrote, and Peter made it clear that the apostates were not God's sheep, but were instead pigs and dogs (2 Peter 2:21-22). The sow had been cleaned on the outside, and the dog on the inside, but neither had been given that new nature which is characteristic of God's true children (2 Peter 1:3-4).

Here, then, we have the "spiritual army" that Jude was addressing. If you have trusted Jesus Christ, you are in this army. God is not looking for volunteers; He has already enlisted you! The question is not "Shall I become a soldier?" Rather, it is, "Will I be a *loyal* soldier?"

Isaac Watts once preached a sermon on 1 Corinthians 16:13: "Watch ye, stand fast in the faith, quit you [act] like men, be strong." When he published the sermon, he added a poem to it; we sing it today as one of our spiritual songs.

> Am I a soldier of the Cross,
> A follower of the Lamb?
> And shall I fear to own His cause,
> Or blush to speak His name?
>
> Must I be carried to the skies
> On flowery beds of ease?
> While others fought to win the prize
> And sailed through bloody seas?

The Enemy (Jude 3-4)
We have already noted that Jude set out to write an encouraging letter about "the common salvation." The name *Jude*

(Judah) means "praise," and he was anxious to praise God and rejoice in the salvation God gives in Jesus Christ. But the Spirit of God changed his mind and led Jude to write about the battle against the forces of evil in the world. Why? Because it was "needful" for the church.

I must confess that I sympathize with Jude. In my own ministry, I would much rather encourage the saints than declare war on the apostates. But when the enemy is in the field, the watchmen dare not go to sleep. The Christian life is a battleground, not a playground.

Jude wasted no time in identifying the enemy.

THEY WERE UNGODLY. This is one of Jude's favorite words. While these men *claimed* to belong to God, they were, in fact, ungodly in their thinking and their living. They might have "a form of godliness," but they lacked the *force* of godliness that lives in the true Christian (2 Tim. 3:5).

THEY WERE DECEITFUL. They "crept in unawares." The Greek word means "to slip in secretly, to steal in under cover." Sometimes Satan's undercover agents are "*brought in* secretly" by those already on the inside (Gal. 2:4), but these men came in on their own. Peter warned that these men were coming (2 Peter 2:1) and now they had arrived on the scene.

How could false brethren get into true assemblies of the saints? *The soldiers had gone to sleep at the post!* The spiritual leaders in the churches had grown complacent and careless. This explains why Jude had to "blow the trumpet" to wake them up. Our Lord and His apostles all warned that false teachers would arise, yet the churches did not heed the warnings. Sad to say, some churches are not heeding the warnings today.

THEY WERE ENEMIES OF GOD'S GRACE. Why did they enter the churches? To attempt to change the doctrine and "turn the grace of our God into lasciviousness" (Jude 4). The word *lasciviousness* simply means "wantonness, absence of moral restraint, indecency." A person who is lascivious thinks *only* of satisfying his lusts, and whatever he touches is stained by his base appetites. Lasciviousness is one of the works of the flesh (Gal. 5:19) that proceeds from the evil heart of man (Mark 7:21-22).

Peter had already warned these people that the apostates would argue, "You have been saved by grace, so you are free to live as you please!" They promised the people freedom, but it was the kind of freedom that led to terrible bondage (2 Peter 2:13-14, 19). The readers both Peter and Jude addressed knew what Paul had written (2 Peter 3:15-16), so they should have been fortified with Romans 6 and 1 Corinthians 5—6.

The apostates, like the cultists today, use the Word of God to promote and defend their false doctrines. They seduce young, immature Christians who have not yet been grounded in the Scriptures. Every soldier of the Cross needs to go through "basic training" in a local church so that he knows how to use the weapons of spiritual warfare (2 Cor. 10:4-5).

THEY DENIED GOD'S TRUTH. "Even denying the Lord that bought them," Peter had warned (2 Peter 2:1). Jude was not writing about two different persons when he wrote "the only Lord God, and our Lord Jesus Christ" for the Greek construction demands that these two names refer to one Person. In other words, Jude was affirming strongly the deity of Jesus Christ. Jesus Christ is God!

But the apostates would deny this. They would agree that Jesus Christ was a good man and a great teacher, but not that He was eternal God come in human flesh. The first test of any religious teacher, as we have seen, is, "What do you think of Jesus Christ? Is He God come in the flesh?" Anyone who denies this cardinal doctrine is a false teacher *no matter how correct he may be in other matters.* If he denies the deity of Christ, something will always be missing in whatever he affirms.

THEY WERE ORDAINED TO JUDGMENT. Jude did not write that these men were ordained to become apostates, as though God were responsible for their sin. They became apostates because they willfully turned away from the truth. But God did ordain that such people would be judged and condemned. The Old Testament prophets denounced the false prophets of their day, and both Jesus Christ and His apostles pronounced judgment on them.

Why should these men be judged by God? To begin with, they had denied His Son! That is reason enough for their condemnation! But they had also defiled God's people by teaching them that God's grace permitted them to practice sin. Furthermore, they derided the doctrine of Christ's coming (2 Peter 3). "Where is the promise of His coming?" They mocked the very promise of Christ's coming and the judgment He would bring against the ungodly.

Of course, they did all these things under the guise of religion, and this made their sin even greater. They deceived innocent people so that they might take their money and enjoy it in godless living. Jesus compared them to wolves in sheep's clothing (Matt. 7:15).

How, then, should the church respond to the presence of this insidious enemy? *By earnestly contending for the faith.*

"The faith" refers to that body of doctrine that was given by God through the apostles to the church. The word *doctrine* is found at least sixteen times in the Pastoral Epistles alone. Paul admonished both Timothy and Titus to make sure the believers were being taught "sound doctrine," which means "healthy doctrine," doctrine that promotes the spiritual health of the local church. While individual teachers and preachers may disagree on the fine points of theology, there is a basic body of truth to which all true Christians are committed.

This body of truth was *delivered* (Jude 3) to the saints. The word means "to be entrusted with." The church collectively, and each Christian personally, has a stewardship to fulfill. "But as we were allowed of God to be put in trust with the Gospel, even so we speak" (1 Thes. 2:4). God committed the truth to Paul (1 Tim. 1:11), and he shared it with others, such as Timothy (1 Tim. 6:20). He exhorted Timothy to entrust the Word to other faithful men (2 Tim. 2:2). You and I would not have the Word today were it not for faithful believers down through the ages who guarded this precious deposit and invested it in others.

The church is always one generation short of extinction. If *our* generation fails to guard the truth and entrust it to our children, then that will be the end! When you think of the saints and martyrs who suffered and died so that we might have God's truth, it makes you want to take your place in God's army and be faithful unto death.

What does it mean to "contend for the faith"? The Greek word is an athletic term that gives us our English word *agonize*. It is the picture of a devoted athlete, competing in the Greek games and stretching his nerves and muscles to do his very best to win. You never fight the Lord's battles from a rocking chair or a soft bed! Both the soldier and the athlete must concentrate on doing their best and giving their all. There must also be teamwork, believers working together to attack and defeat the enemy.

Sometimes you hear well-meaning people say, "Well, it's fine to contend for the faith, but don't be so contentious!" While it is true that some of God's soldiers have been the cause of quarrels and divisions, it is also true that some of them have paid a great price to defend the faith. As Christian soldiers, we must not fight each other or go around locking for trouble. But when the banner of Christ is in danger of being taken by the enemy, we cannot sit idly by, nor can we ever hope to win the victory by wearing kid gloves.

Charles Spurgeon once said that "the new views are not the old truth in a better dress, but deadly errors with which we can have no fellowship." False doctrine is a deadly poison that must be identified, labeled, and avoided. Spurgeon also said, "I cannot endure false doctrine, however neatly it may be put before me. Would you have me eat poisoned meat because the dish is of the choicest ware?"

We must always speak the truth in love, and the weapons we use must be spiritual. At the same time, we must dare to take our stand for "the faith" even if our stand offends some and upsets others. We are not fighting personal enemies, but the enemies of the Lord. It is the honor and glory of Jesus Christ that is at stake. "Fight the good fight of faith" (1 Tim. 6:12).

The Victory (Jude 5-7)
Like the Apostle Peter, Jude reached back into Old Testament history and gave three examples of God's victory over those who had resisted his authority and turned from the truth. Peter referred to the fallen angels, Noah, and Lot (2 Peter 2:4-9) and followed the historical order. He also emphasized God's deliverance of the righteous as well as His judgment of the ungodly. Jude, however, did not mention Noah and the flood, but instead used the nation Israel as his example.

The point Jude was making is that *God judges apostates.* Therefore, the false teachers who had crept into the church would also one day be judged. Their seeming success would not last; God would have the last word.

ISRAEL (v. 5). Both Paul (1 Cor. 10) and the author of

Hebrews (chapters 3—4) used the experiences of Israel to illustrate important spiritual truths. The nation was delivered from Egypt by the power of God and brought to the border of the Promised Land. But the people were afraid and did not have the faith to enter in and possess the land (see Num. 13—14). Moses, Joshua, and Caleb tried to encourage the people to obey God by faith, but the people refused. In fact, the leaders of the tribes even wanted to organize and go back to Egypt, the place of bondage!

This was rebellion against the will and the Word of God, and God cannot tolerate rebellion. As a result, everybody in the camp twenty years and older was destined to die at some time in the next forty years. Their unbelief led to their extermination.

Keep in mind that Jude was using an historical event as an illustration, and we must not press every detail. The entire nation was delivered from Egypt, but that does not mean that each individual was personally saved through faith in the Lord. The main point of the account is that privileges bring responsibilities, and God cannot lightly pass over the sins of His people. If any of Jude's readers dared to follow the false teachers, they too would face the discipline of God. "Wherefore let him that thinketh he standeth take heed lest he fall" (1 Cor. 10:12).

THE FALLEN ANGELS (v. 6). We studied this illustration in 2 Peter 2:4, but Jude seems to add a new dimension to it by associating the fall of the angels with the destruction of Sodom and Gomorrah (Jude 7, "even as . . . in like manner"). Some Bible students believe that Jude was teaching not only a revolt of the angels against God, but also an invasion of earth by these fallen angels. They point to Genesis 6:1-4 and claim that "the sons of God" were fallen angels who assumed human bodies, cohabited with the daughters of men, and produced a race of giants on the earth. This was one reason that God sent the Flood.

As attractive and popular as this view is, I must confess that I have a difficult time accepting it. It is true that "the sons of God" is a title for angels (Job 1:6; 2:1; 38:7), but always for *unfallen* angels. Would the Holy Spirit, writing through Moses, call *rebellious* angels "the sons of God"? I doubt it.

My second problem is that angels are spirits and do not have bodies. In the Old Testament record, we do read of angels who *appeared* in human form, but this was not incarnation. How could a spirit being have a physical relationship with a woman, even if that being assumed a temporary body of some kind? Our Lord taught that the angels were sexless (Matt. 22:30).

Third, it appears that God sent the Flood because of what *man* did, not what angels did. "My spirit shall not always strive with *man*. . . . And God saw that the wickedness of *man* was great in the earth. . . . And it repented [grieved] the Lord that He had made *man* on the earth" (Gen. 6:3, 5-6, italics mine). If this "fallen angel" view is correct, God should have repented that He created *the angels!*

Fourth, the phrases "even as" and "in like manner" in verse 7 need not be interpreted to say that the angels did what the Sodomites did, namely, "going after strange flesh." Notice the grammatical connections in the verse, and you will get the message: "Even as Sodom and Gomorrah . . . in like manner . . . are set forth for an example." The angels are an example of God's judgment and so are Sodom and Gomorrah.

I might add that Genesis 6:4 presents a strong argument *against* the view that fallen angels cohabited with women and produced a race of giants. "There were giants in the earth in those days; *and also after that*" (italics mine). This would mean that a *second* invasion of fallen angels had to take place! We have no record of this in Scripture.

Finally, both Peter and Jude state clearly that these rebellious angels are chained in darkness and reserved for judgment. They would have to have invaded the earth *prior* to being arrested and chained by God. We wonder why God would have permitted them to "run loose" long enough to get the women into sin and help to cause the great Flood. The whole explanation, though held by teachers whom I respect, to me seems a bit fantastic. The simplest explanation of Genesis 6 is that the godly line of Seth ("the sons of God") began to mingle with the ungodly line of Cain, and this broke down the walls of separation, resulting in compromise and eventually degrading sin. But regardless of which interpretation you accept, keep the main lesson in mind: the angels rebelled and were punished for their rebellion.

SODOM AND GOMORRAH (v. 7). Both Peter and Jude state that God made these cities an example to warn the ungodly that God does indeed judge sin (see 2 Peter 2:6). When you combine their descriptions, you discover that the citizens of Sodom and Gomorrah (and the other cities involved) were: ungodly, filthy, wicked, unlawful, unjust, and given over to fornication. They did not *occasionally* commit unnatural sexual sins; they indulged in them and gave themselves over to the pursuit of lust. The Greek verb is intensive: "to indulge in excessive immorality." This was their way of life—and death!

Strange flesh means "different flesh." The bent of their life was constantly downward, indulging in unnatural acts (see Rom. 1:24-27). Those who hold the "fallen angel" interpretation of Genesis 6 make the "strange flesh" refer to angels in human form; but when did the angels invade Sodom and Gomorrah? And, if fallen angels are meant, how can their sin and the sin of the Sodomites apply to us today, for we have no fallen angels to tempt or seduce us? Indeed, the men at Lot's door did want to engage in homosexual activity with his angelic guests, but the Sodomites did not know they were angels. Another possibility is that the Sodomites were guilty not only of unnatural sex with each other, but also with animals, which would be "strange flesh." Both homosexuality and beastiality are condemned by God (Lev. 18:22-25).

These cities were *set forth* by God as an example and warning to ungodly people today. The verb *set forth* means "to expose openly to public view." (Interestingly enough, the word was used to describe a corpse lying in state!) But the cities of the plain are not *today* in public view. It is generally agreed among archeologists that Sodom and Gomorrah are buried under the southern end of the Dead Sea. How, then, do they serve as an example? *In the pages of the Word of God.* No one can read Genesis 18—19 without clearly seeing God's hatred for sin and, at the same time, His patience and willingness to postpone judgment. This certainly ties in with Peter's explanation for God's seeming delay in fulfilling the promise of Christ's return (2 Peter 3:8ff).

The sin of Israel was rebellious unbelief (Heb. 3:12). The sin of the angels was rebellion against the throne of God. The sin of Sodom and Gomorrah was indulging in unnatural lust. Unbelief, rebellion against authority, and sensual indulgence were sins characteristic of the false teachers. The conclusion is obvious: the apostates will be judged. But, meanwhile, God's soldiers must stay on duty and see to it that these false teachers do not creep into the ranks and start to lead people astray. "Take heed unto thyself, and unto the doctrine" (1 Tim. 4:16).

What can we do practically to oppose the enemy and maintain the purity and unity of the church? For one thing, we must know the Word of God and have the courage to defend it. Every local church ought to be a Bible institute, and every Christian ought to be a Bible student. The pulpit needs to declare positive truth as well as denounce error.

Second, we must "watch and pray." The enemy is already here and we dare not go to sleep! Spiritual leaders in local congregations need to be alert as they interview candidates for baptism and church membership. Committees need to seek the mind of Christ as they appoint Sunday School teachers, youth sponsors, and other church leaders. Congregations must exercise discernment as they select officers.

Third, congregations and members must be careful where they send their money. "Should you help the wicked and love those who hate the Lord?" (See 2 Chron. 19:2.)

Finally, we must have the courage to maintain a position of biblical separation from those who deny Christ and the fundamental doctrines of the Word (Rom. 16:17-20; 2 Tim. 2:15ff; 2 John 6-11). This does not mean that we separate from fellow believers over minor doctrinal differences, or that we practice "guilt by association." God's true army needs to stand together in the battle for truth.

Have you heeded the call to arms?

11

Meet
the Apostates!

Jude 8-16

Jude was not content simply to remind his readers to pay attention to what Peter had written. He wanted to add his own words of warning by describing what the false teachers were like and what they would do to the church. The Spirit of God led Jude to describe the characteristics of the apostates, reinforcing Peter's words and, at the same time, adding information. Jude 8-16 and 2 Peter 2 parallel and supplement each other.

But why this seemingly needless repetition? The Apostle Paul gave the answer: "To write the same things to you, to me indeed is not grievous, but for you it is safe" (Phil. 3:1). Parents repeat warnings and instructions to their children, and sometimes the children reply, "I know that! You've already told me a million times!" But wise parents know that some things *must* be said again and again for the safety and welfare of their children—whether the children want to hear them or not!

All that Jude wrote about the apostates in these verses may be summarized in three statements.

They Reject Divine Authority (Jude 8-11)

All authority comes from the throne of God, whether it is authority in the home, the church, or the state. Those who exercise authority must first be *under* authority, accountable to God. But the false teachers reject divine authority and set themselves up as their own authority.

The *cause* of their rebellion is found in the word *dreamers* (v. 8). These people live in a dreamworld of unreality and delusion. They believe Satan's lie, "Ye shall be as gods" (Gen. 3:5). Having turned away from God's truth, they feed their minds on false doctrine that inflates their egos and encourages their rebellion. Verse 10 informs us that the apostates are ignorant people who do not know what they are talking about! Jude echoed Peter's description of these men as "brute beasts" (2 Peter 2:12, 22). Animals live by natural instinct, and so do the apostates. When men rebel against God, they sink to the level of beasts.

The *course* of their rebellion was clearly described by Jude. As a result of their rebellion and pride, they "defile the flesh," living to satisfy their animal lusts. When a person despises God's authority, he feels free to disobey God's laws and live as he pleases. What he forgets is that those laws have penalties attached to them so that he cannot disobey and escape the consequences.

They also use their tongues to express their rebellion against God. "With our tongue will we prevail; our lips are our own: who is lord over us?" (Ps. 12:4) The phrase *speak evil* in verses 8 and 10 simply means "to blaspheme." Blasphemy involves much more than taking God's name in vain, though that is at the heart of it. A person blasphemes God when he takes His Word lightly and even jests about it, or when he deliberately defies God to judge him. "They set their mouth against the heavens, and their tongue walketh through the earth. And they say, 'How doth God know? and is there knowledge in the Most High?' " (Ps. 73:9, 11)

The *consequence* of their rebellion is seen in their own ruin: "they corrupt [destroy] themselves" (Jude 10). They defile themselves (v. 8) and they destroy themselves, yet they have the idea they are promoting themselves! "Because sentence against an evil work is not executed speedily, therefore the heart of the sons of men is fully set in them to do evil" (Ecc. 8:11). The way of rebellion is but the way to ruin.

Arrogant speech is a dangerous thing, and so is despising the authority that God has established. Even the Archangel Michael (Dan. 10:13) did not dare to rebuke Satan, but respected the authority given to him by God. The name *Michael* means "Who is like God?" Ironically, Satan had said in his rebellion, "I will be like the Most High!" (Isa. 14:14), and his offer to men is, "Ye shall be as gods" (Gen. 3:5).

We have no information about the conflict between Satan and Michael over the body of Moses. When Moses died, the Lord buried him and no one knew where the sepulchre was located (Deut. 34:5-6). No doubt the Jewish people would have made a shrine out of the sepulchre and fallen into idolatry, so God kept the information to Himself. The text tells us that "not any man" knew the place, so perhaps Satan did know the place and tried to claim Moses' body for himself. Inasmuch as Satan does have a certain amount of authority in the realm of death he may have felt he had a right to interfere (Heb. 2:14-15).

The point is that Michael did not rebuke Satan, but left that to the Lord. It is a dangerous thing for God's people to confront Satan directly and to argue with him, because he is much stronger than we are. If an archangel is careful about the way he deals with the devil, how much more cautious ought we to be! While it is true that we share in the victory of Christ, it is also true that we must not be presumptuous. Satan is a dangerous enemy, and when we resist him, we must be sober and vigilant (1 Peter 5:8-9).

"The Lord rebuke thee!" has a parallel in Zechariah 3:1-5. The prophet had a vision of the high priest standing before God's throne in defiled garments, symbolizing the sinful condition of the nation Israel after the Babylonian captivity. Satan had every right to accuse the people (see Rev. 12:9-11), except for one thing: they were the chosen ones of God, His covenant people, and He would not go back on His Word. God forgave His people, gave them clean garments, and warned them to walk in His ways. This is an Old Testament illustration of 1 John 1:5—2:2.

The *condemnation* of the false teachers is given in Jude 11: "Woe unto them!" Jude cited three examples from the Old Testament to illustrate the enormity of their sins, three men who rebelled against God's authority and who suffered for it.

Cain rebelled against God's way of salvation (Gen. 4; 1 John 3:11-12). By clothing Adam and Eve with the skins of slain animals (Gen. 3:21), God made it clear that the only way of forgiveness is through the shedding of blood. This is the way of faith, not the way of good works (Eph. 2:8-10). But Cain rejected this divinely authorized way and came to the altar with the fruits of his own labor. God rejected Cain's offering because God rejected Cain: his heart was not right before God. It was *by faith* that Abel's sacrifice was offered, and that was why God accepted it (Heb. 11:4).

The "way of Cain" is the way of religion without faith, righteousness based on character and good works. The "way of Cain" is the way of pride, a man establishing his own righteousness and rejecting the righteousness of God that comes through faith in Christ (Rom. 10:1-4; Phil. 3:3-12). Cain became a fugitive and tried to overcome his wretchedness by building a city and developing a civilization (Gen. 4:9ff). He ended up with everything a man could desire everything except God, that is.

We have already studied "the way of Balaam" (see 2 Peter 2:15-16). The "way of Balaam" is merchandising one's gifts and ministry just for the purpose of making money. It is using the spiritual to gain the material (see 1 Thes. 2:5-6; 1 Tim. 6:3-21). The false teachers were greedy for material gain and, like Balaam, would do anything for money. The "error of Balaam" is thinking that they can get away with this kind of rebellion. Balaam was a true prophet of God, but he prostituted his gifts and sought to destroy God's people. God turned Balaam's curses into blessings (Deut. 23: 4-5).

While we are on the subject of Balaam, we might note the "doctrine of Balaam" (Rev. 2:14) which is, "You can violate your separated position and get away with it!" He told King Balak that the fastest way to destroy Israel would be to corrupt the nation by having the people defile themselves with the heathen nations around them. "You are God's chosen people," was the argument. "Certainly a little friendship with your neighbors will not hurt you!" It was "turning the grace of . . . God into lasciviousness" (Jude 4), and God judged both Israel and Balaam.

The story of Core (Korah) is found in Numbers 16, and it too centers on rebellion against authority. Korah and his followers resented the leadership of Moses and dared God to do anything about their rebellion. In speaking against ("gainsaying") Moses, they were speaking against the Lord who had given Moses his authority. This is a warning to us today, for it is so easy to speak against spiritual or governmental leaders in a careless way (see Titus 3:1-2). God judged Korah and his followers and established clearly the authority of His servant, Moses.

Cain rebelled against God's authority in *salvation*, for he refused to bring a blood sacrifice as God had commanded.

Balaam rebelled against God's authority in *separation*, for he prostituted his gifts for money and led Israel to mix with the other nations. Korah rebelled against God's authority in *service*, denying that Moses was God's appointed servant and attempting to usurp his authority.

It is interesting to note the verbs that Jude used in this verse. The apostates "traveled on the road" of Cain, "gave themselves over to" the error of Balaam, and "perished" in the rebellion of Korah. The tragedy of rejecting authority!

They Resort to Deliberate Hypocrisy (Jude 12-13, 16)

Verses 12 and 13 present six vivid pictures of the false teachers and help to explain why they are dangerous to the church.

FILTHY SPOTS. Peter called them spots and blemishes (2 Peter 2:13). These men had invaded the "love feasts" in the local assemblies, but all they did was defile them. Instead of adding to the sanctity of the occasion, they detracted from it, like Judas at the last Passover that Jesus celebrated with His disciples. The tragedy is that the members of the assembly did not realize the true character of these men! They thought the men were spiritual!

The Greek word translated *spots* can also mean "hidden rocks." The mariner who is unaware of the hidden rocks can quickly wreck his ship. The pilot must always be alert, for waters that look calm and safe can contain treacherous reefs. Spiritual leaders must constantly be on guard.

SELFISH SHEPHERDS. The word translated *feeding* means "shepherding." Instead of shepherding the flock and caring for the needs of the people, these apostates only take care of themselves. Jude may have had in mind Isaiah 56:10-12 and Ezekiel 34, where the prophets condemned the political and spiritual leaders of the nation ("shepherds") for exploiting the people and caring only for themselves.

It is a serious thing to be a shepherd over God's flock. Our example must be Jesus Christ, the Good Shepherd who gave His life for the sheep. False shepherds *use* and *abuse* people in order to get what they want, and yet all the while, *the people love it!* Paul marveled at this when he wrote 2 Corinthians 11:20—"You don't mind, do you, if a man takes away your liberty, spends your money, takes advantage of you, puts on airs, or even smacks your face?" (PH)

These selfish shepherds do all of this "without fear." They are an arrogant lot! This is the difference between a true shepherd and a hireling: the true shepherd cares for the sheep, while the hireling cares only for himself. "Woe be to the shepherds of Israel that do feed themselves! Should not the shepherds feed the flocks?" (Ezek. 34:2) But these apostates *ought* to be afraid, for their judgment is coming.

EMPTY CLOUDS. Clouds that promise rain, but fail to produce, are a disappointment to the farmer whose crops desperately need water. The apostates look like men who can give spiritual help, and they boast of their abilities, but they are unable to produce. "Whoso boasteth himself of a false gift [a gift he does not give] is like clouds and wind without rain" (Prov. 25:14). They promise liberty, but they can only give bondage (2 Peter 2:19).

The Word of God is sometimes compared to the rain and the dew. "My doctrine shall drop as the rain, my speech shall distill as the dew" (Deut. 32:2). Isaiah 55:10 compares God's Word to the rain and snow from heaven that bring fruit on the earth. Like the clouds in the sky, the false teachers may be prominent and even attractive; but if they cannot bring rain, they are useless.

DEAD TREES. The picture is that of an orchard in autumn, the time when the farmer expects fruit. But these trees are fruitless! "Ye shall know them by their fruits" (Matt. 7:16). Those who teach and preach the Word have the responsibility of feeding others, but the false teachers have nothing to give. Not only are they fruitless, but they are also rootless ("plucked up by the root"); this is why they are "twice dead." What a contrast to the godly man in Psalm 1:3!

One of the evidences of true salvation is producing spiritual fruit. The seed that fell on the hard soil, the shallow soil, and the crowded soil did not produce fruit; but the seed that fell on the "good ground" did produce fruit (Matt. 13:1-9, 18-23). No matter how much of the Bible the false teachers may quote, the seed is not producing fruit in their own lives or through their ministries. Why? Because they have no spiritual roots. They lack spiritual life.

Fruit has in it the seed for more fruit (Gen. 1:11-12). One of the evidences that a ministry is truly of God is that the fruit multiplies. Manufactured "results" are sterile and dead, but true fruit continues to grow and reproduce itself in the lives of others.

RAGING WAVES. I personally do not enjoy being *in* or *on* the ocean (I am not a good swimmer). However, I do enjoy sitting *by* the ocean and contemplating its grandeur and power. But I certainly would not want to be either in or on the ocean in a storm! There is great power in those waves, as many a mariner has discovered. But Jude compares the apostates to "raging waves of the sea" not because of their power, but because of their pride and arrogant speech. "Their mouth speaketh great swelling words" (v. 16). Like the swelling of the sea, they make a lot of noise, *but what do they produce?* Have you ever walked along the beach the morning after a storm and seen the ugly refuse that has been deposited on the shore?

Jude may have had Isaiah 57:20 in mind: "But the wicked are like the troubled sea, when it cannot rest, whose waters cast up mire and dirt." All that the "great swelling words" of the apostates can produce is foam and flotsam! The true teachers of the Word bring up the treasures of the deep, but the false teachers produce only refuse. And what they boast about, they really ought to be ashamed of! (See Phil. 3:19.)

WANDERING STARS. Jude was not referring to fixed stars, planets, or comets, because they have definite positions and orbits. He was referring to meteors, falling stars that suddenly appear and then vanish into the darkness, never to be seen again. Our Lord is compared to a star (Rev. 2:28; 22:16), and Christians are to shine as stars in this dark world (Phil. 2:15). Fixed stars can be depended on to guide the traveler through the darkness, but wandering stars can only lead him astray.

One of my hobbies is collecting books of sermons, not only by famous preachers, but also by obscure and forgotten men whose names once were famous. I have noticed that many a "pulpit beacon" has turned out to be a fallen star! It is disturbing to read histories and biographies and see how "the mighty have fallen." For the most part, those who have been true to the Word are ministering yet today as lights shining in the darkness, while the preachers of false doctrine have fallen into oblivion.

God has reserved chains of darkness for the rebellious angels (Jude 6), and He has reserved "the blackness of darkness forever" for apostate teachers. Beware of following a falling star! It will lead you into eternal blackness!

As you review these six pictures of the false teachers, you can easily see how dangerous they are and how important it is for the church to keep them out. Verse 16 completes the description and emphasizes even more why they are so dangerous: they are out to please themselves by taking advantage of others. This reminds us of Peter's statement (2 Peter 2:14), "A heart they have exercised with covetous practices," or, as Phillips translates it, "Their technique of getting what they want is, through long practice, highly developed." They give the impression that they are out to help you, but they are interested only in gratifying their own lusts.

What is their approach? For one thing, they murmur and complain and cause people to become dissatisfied with life. While each of us should do all we can, as God enables us, to improve our lot in life, at the same time we must be careful not to criticize God's providences or hinder His plans. The nation Israel was judged because of her complaining (1 Cor. 10:1-10), and Christians are commanded not to complain (Phil. 2:14-16). If a false teacher can make a person critical of his pastor or church, or dissatisfied with his situation, he then can lead him astray into false doctrine.

The false teachers also use "great swelling words" to impress ignorant people. Peter called their speeches "great swelling words of vanity" (2 Peter 2:18). They impress people with their vocabularies and oratory, but what they say is just so much "hot air." They also use flattery to manipulate their listeners. They "bow and scrape" and pay compliments to others, *if* it is to their advantage.

Knowing these things, we are amazed that anybody would listen to these apostates and follow them; but many people are doing it today! There is something in fallen human nature that loves a lie and is willing to follow it, no matter where it may lead. But the success of the apostates is only temporary, for their judgment is coming.

They Receive Their Due Penalty (Jude 14-15)

All that we know about Enoch from Scripture is found in Genesis 5:18-24, Hebrews 11:5, and these two verses in Jude. He is called "the seventh from Adam" to identify him as the *godly* Enoch, since Cain had a son of the same name (Gen. 4:17). In a society that was rapidly being polluted and destroyed by sin, Enoch walked with God and kept his life clean. He also ministered as a prophet and announced the coming judgment.

Bible scholars tell us that this quotation is from an apocryphal book called *The Book of Enoch*. The fact that Jude quoted from this nonbiblical book does not mean the book is inspired and trustworthy, any more than Paul's quotations from the Greek poets put God's "seal of approval" on everything they wrote. The Spirit of God led Jude to use this quotation and make it a part of the inspired Scriptures.

When Enoch originally gave this message, it is possible that he was also referring to the coming judgment of the Flood. He certainly lived in an ungodly age, and it seemed that sinners were getting away with their evil deeds. But Enoch made it clear that judgment was coming and that the ungodly would get what was coming to them!

However, the final application of this prophecy is to the world in the end times, the very judgment that Peter wrote about in 2 Peter 3. The false teachers mocked this prophecy and argued that Jesus Christ would never come and God would never send judgment. But their very attitude was proof that the Word is true, for both our Lord and His apostles, as well as the prophets, said that scoffers and mockers would appear in the last days (2 Peter 3:1-4). Enoch gave his prophecy thousands of years ago! See how patient God has been with those who have rebelled against Him!

What does Enoch's prophecy say about the coming judgment? It will be a *personal* judgment: God Himself will come to judge the world. He will not send a famine or a flood, nor will He assign the task to an angel. He Himself will come. This shows the seriousness of the event, and also its finality. "Behold, the judge standeth before the door" (James 5:9).

Though it is a personal judgment, our Lord will not judge alone; the saints of God will be with Him. The word *saints* in Jude 14 means "holy ones" and can also refer to the angels (Deut. 33:2; Matt. 25:31). However, we know from Revelation 19:14, Colossians 3:4, and 1 Thessalonians 3:13 that the people of God will accompany the Lord when He returns to earth to defeat His enemies and establish His righteous kingdom (cf. 1 Cor. 6:2-3). Over the centuries, the people of God have suffered at the hands of the ungodly, but one day the tables will be turned.

It will be a *universal* judgment. He will execute judgment "upon all"—none will escape. Just as the Flood destroyed all who were outside the ark, and the fire and brimstone destroyed all in Sodom and Gomorrah except Lot and his wife and two daughters, so the last judgment will encompass all the ungodly. The word *ungodly* is used four times in this one verse! It will be "the day of judgment and perdition [ruin, destruction] of ungodly men" (2 Peter 3:7).

It will be a *just* judgment. God will convict ("convince") them of their sins, declare them guilty, pass sentence on them, and then execute the punishment. There will be a judge, Jesus Christ (John 5:22), but no jury. There will be prosecution, but no defense; for every mouth will be stopped (Rom. 3:19). There will be a sentence, but no appeal, for there can be no higher court than God's final judgment. The entire procedure will be just, for the righteous Son of God will be in charge.

The Lord will have the record of their "ungodly deeds." He will also have a record of their motives and hidden desires as they committed these deeds and even these will be ungodly! He will recall the "hard speeches" (Jude 15) that they uttered against the Lord. The word *hard* carries the idea of "rough, harsh, stern, uncivil." After all, these people were "murmurers" and "complainers" (v. 16) and spoke harsh things against God. They were not "afraid to speak evil of dignities" (2 Peter 2:10), but at the judgment, their words will testify against them. They spoke "great swelling words" (2 Peter 2:18; Jude 16), but at the judgment, their great words will bring great wrath.

There are times when God's children ask, "Lord, how long shall the wicked, how long shall the wicked triumph? How long shall they utter and speak hard things? and all the workers of iniquity boast themselves?" (Ps. 94:3-4) The answer is given in Psalm 50:3—"Our God shall come, and shall not keep silence: a fire shall devour before Him, and it shall be very tempestuous round about Him."

The words are familiar, but what James Russell Lowell wrote in "The Present Crisis" certainly applies today.

> Careless seems the great Avenger; history's pages
> but record
> One death-grapple in the darkness 'twix old
> systems and the Word;
> Truth forever on the scaffold, Wrong forever on
> the throne—
> Yet that scaffold sways the future, and, behind the
> dim unknown,
> Standeth God within the shadow, keeping watch
> above His own. . . .

"Nevertheless we, according to His promise, look for new heavens and a new earth, wherein dwelleth righteousness" (2 Peter 3:13).

"Even so, come, Lord Jesus!"

12
You Don't Have to Stumble
Jude 17-25

I read somewhere that the Great Wall of China was penetrated at least three times by the enemy, and each time the guards were bribed!

A strong defense depends on strong people, and this applies to spiritual battles as well as military contests. If the church is to oppose and defeat the false teachers, then all of us in the church must be strong and able to "stand against the wiles of the devil" (Eph. 6:11). There is always the danger of stumbling (Jude 24) and a stumble is the first step toward a fall.

In this closing paragraph, Jude addressed his beloved readers and gave them four instructions to follow if they would stand firm and resist the apostates.

Remember God's Word (Jude 17-19)
From the very beginning, Satan has attacked the Word of God. "Yea, hath God said?" was his opening thrust when he led Eve into disobedience in the garden (Gen. 3:1). Once we begin to question God's Word, we are vulnerable to Satan's

other attacks, for only the truth of the Word can protect us from the lies of the devil. "To the law and to the testimony: if they speak not according to this Word, it is because there is no light in them" (Isa. 8:20).

REMEMBER WHO GAVE THE WORD (v. 17). While our Lord had many disciples, He selected only a few to be *apostles*. The word means "one who is sent with a commission." In order to qualify, a believer had to be a witness of the resurrection of Christ (1 Cor. 9:1; Acts 1:21-22). The apostles lived with Christ during His ministry, learned from Him, and were sent by Him into all the world to carry the Good News of salvation.

Wherever there is the authentic, the counterfeit will appear; this happened in the early church. False apostles and teachers began to appear, and it was necessary to develop a system to protect the church against false prophecies and forged letters. Since Christ had committed "the faith" (Jude 3) to His apostles, one of the main tests in the early church was, "Is this what the apostles taught?" When the church assembled the New Testament books, it was required that each book be written either by an apostle or by someone closely associated with an apostle. Apostolic teaching was, and still is, the test of truth.

Jude mentioned the words that were "spoken" by the apostles, because originally there were no New Testament epistles. Over the years, inspired letters were written by Paul, Peter, and John; we have these letters in our New Testament. We also have a record of some of their sermons in the Book of Acts. We no longer depend on tradition since we have the completed Scriptures, both the Old Testament and the New.

Whenever somebody offers you a "new revelation," test it by what the apostles wrote and by what Jesus Christ taught. You will soon discover that the "revelation" is a lie.

REMEMBER WHAT THEY SAID (v. 18). They prophesied that, in these last days, mockers would come who would deny the Word of God. Jude echoed what Peter had written (2 Peter 3:3ff), but Paul and John also warned their readers about the apostates (1 Tim. 4; 2 Tim. 3; 1 John 2:18ff; 4:1-6). When a warning is given so many times, it behooves us to take it seriously!

The phrase "walking after their own lusts" appears in 2 Peter 3:3 and Jude 16 and 18, and it explains *why* the apostates deny God's truth: they do not want God to tell them how to live. They want to satisfy their own sinful desires, and the Word of God condemns their selfish way of life. When a person says, "I have intellectual problems with the Bible," he probably has *moral* problems because the Bible contradicts what he is doing. The only sure way to know the truth of the Bible is by obeying it (John 7:17).

Before Satan can substitute his own lies, he must get rid of the truth of God's Word. If he cannot argue it away, he will laugh it away, and he can usually find somebody to laugh with him.

REMEMBER WHY THEY SAID IT (v. 19). The false teachers want to divide the church and lead people out of the true fellowship into their false fellowship. "Also of your own selves shall men arise, speaking perverse things, to draw away disciples after them" (Acts 20:30). Their appeal is usually, "We have a deeper knowledge of the Word that your church doesn't have! We have a better understanding of prophecy, or of the Christian life, than you do." They offer a "higher quality" religion than that of the apostles.

Not only do false teachers divide the church, but they also deceive the church, because they are "sensual, having not the Spirit." The word *sensual* means the opposite of "spiritual." This is the way Paul used it in 1 Corinthians 2:14-16, where it is translated "natural." (The Greek word is *psukikos*, which means "soulish.") Because the false teachers do not have the Spirit of God, they must function on their natural "soul power" alone.

One of the tragedies in ministry today is that some of God's people cannot discern between "soul ministry" and the true ministry of the Spirit. There is so much "religious showmanship" these days that the saints are confused and deceived. Just as there was "false fire" in the tabernacle (Lev. 10), so there is "false fire" today in the church; therefore we must exercise careful discernment.

How can we discern between the "soulish" and the "spiritual"? By using the Word of God which is able to divide soul and spirit (Heb. 4:12); and by paying close attention to the witness of the Spirit of God within (Rom. 8:16). A "soulish" ministry magnifies man, but the Spirit glorifies Jesus Christ. When the Spirit is ministering through the Word, there is edification; but when the soul is merely "manufacturing" a ministry, there is entertainment or, at best, only intellectual education. It takes the Spirit of God to minister to our spirits and to make us more like Jesus Christ.

Build Your Christian Life (Jude 20-21)
The Christian life must never stand still; if it does, it will go backward. A house left to itself falls apart. The apostates are in the business of tearing down, but each Christian must be involved in building up—first, his own spiritual life and then his local assembly.

The foundation for our Christian life is our "most holy faith" (v. 20), which is the same as "the faith which was once delivered unto the saints" (v. 3). There is a sense, of course, in which our faith in Jesus Christ is the basis for our growth, but even that faith depends on what God has revealed to us in His Word. Subjective faith depends on objective revelation of truth.

The Word of God is certainly central in spiritual growth. I have yet to meet a strong, fruitful Christian who ignores his Bible. We must daily spend devotional time in the Word, seeking the mind of God. We must also study the Word regularly, in a disciplined way, so that we better understand what it teaches. The gifted Chinese preacher, Watchman Nee, used to read through the New Testament once a month. This becomes apparent when you read his books, for you are struck with his wonderful insights into God's Word. The members of the Chinese church used to have a saying, "No Bible—no breakfast!" If we followed that motto in America, I wonder how many Christians would go hungry.

The power for building the Christian life comes from prayer: "praying in the Holy Ghost" (v. 20). The Word of God and prayer go together in spiritual growth. If all we do is read and study the Bible, we will have a great deal of light, but not much power. However, if we concentrate on prayer and ignore the Bible, we may be guilty of zeal without knowledge. We read the Word to grow in faith (Rom. 10:17), then we use that faith to ask God for what we need and what His Word tells us we may have.

The Word of God and prayer certainly go together (Acts 6:4). Evangelist Billy Sunday used to give his converts three rules for success in the Christian life. Each day they were to read the Bible and let God talk to them. They were to pray; in other words, they were to talk to God. And they were to witness and talk to others about God. It would be difficult to improve on those rules.

What does it mean to "pray in the Holy Spirit"? (Note the contrast with verse 19—"having not the Spirit.") It means to pray according to the leading of the Spirit. It has well been said, "Prayer is not getting man's will done in heaven—it is getting God's will done on earth." This agrees with 1 John 5:14-15.

As Christians, we may pray in solitude (Matt. 6:6), but we never pray *alone;* the Spirit of God joins with us as we pray (Rom. 8:26-28) because He knows the mind of God and can direct us. He can give us wisdom and knowledge from the Word (Eph. 1:15ff). He can also help us approach the Father through the access we have in Jesus Christ (Eph. 2:18). We worship God "in the Spirit" (Phil. 3:3), and the Spirit motivates us to pray, for He is "the Spirit of grace and of supplications" (Zech. 12:10). When the believer is yielded to the Spirit, then the Spirit will assist him in his prayer life, and God will answer prayer.

This "building process" in the Christian life involves the Word of God, the Spirit of God, and prayer. But these things, as precious as they are, can become somewhat routine; so Jude added another factor: *abiding in God's love* (v. 21). He did not write, "Keep yourselves saved!" because he had already assured them that they were "preserved in Jesus Christ" (v. 1). He wrote, "Keep yourselves in the love of God." Our Lord made a similar statement recounted in John 15:9—"Continue ye in My love."

To love God means much more than to enjoy a special kind of feeling. Of course, as we grow in grace, we do experience deeper fellowship with the Father (John 14:21-24), and we do have times when He seems very near. The Bible compares this to the love of a husband and wife (Eph. 5:22ff). Any happily married couple can tell you that love deepens over the years.

But it takes more than ecstatic feelings to make a successful marriage—or a successful Christian life! There must also be obedience and mutual concern. "But whoso keepeth His Word, in him verily is the love of God perfected" (1 John 2:5). "If ye keep My commandments, ye shall abide in My love" (John 15:10). We grow in our love for God as we listen to His Word, obey it, and delight in doing what pleases Him.

That is how we keep ourselves in God's love.

God's love is a holy love; it is not shallow sentiment. "Ye that love the Lord, hate evil" (Ps. 97:10). To love God is to love what He loves and hate what He hates! We please Him by doing those things that He commands. It is the dedicated, separated Christian who enjoys the deepest fellowship with the Father in the family (2 Cor. 6:14-18).

We build our Christian life on the foundation of faith and through the motivation of love. But we also need hope: "looking for the mercy of our Lord Jesus Christ unto eternal life." The believer's eyes must be lifted heavenward. "Looking for that blessed hope, and the glorious appearing of the great God and our Saviour Jesus Christ" (Titus 2:13). "Looking for and hasting unto the coming of the day of God" (2 Peter 3:12).

The word translated *looking* (Jude 21) means "earnestly expecting." It describes an attitude of life that is motivated by the promise of our Lord's return. The apostates can only look for judgment, but God's people are looking for mercy. Not only is our salvation from sin the gift of God's mercy, but so also is the deliverance of His church from this evil world. In His mercy, He will come for us and take us to Himself.

We have already noted that looking for the coming of the Lord is a great encouragement to Christian living. It makes us want to keep pure (1 John 3:3) and to avoid the things of the flesh and the world (Phil. 3:17-21). Our hope in Christ is like an anchor (Heb. 6:19) that holds us in the storms of life, and like a helmet that protects us in the battles of life (1 Thes. 5:8).

The three "Christian graces" of faith, hope, and love enable us to grow in our spiritual walk. We are able to build on a solid foundation with materials that will not decay. Mere profession with the lips will not suffice. "Not every one that saith unto me, 'Lord, Lord,' shall enter into the kingdom of heaven; but he that doeth the will of My Father which is in heaven" (Matt. 7:21). The Parable of the Two Builders (Matt. 7:24-27) makes it clear that to obey the will of God means to build on a foundation that cannot fail.

Exercise Spiritual Discernment (Jude 22-23)

What should be the attitude of the growing Christian toward those who are being influenced by the apostates? Jude instructed his readers to exercise discernment and to act on the basis of that discernment. He described three different kinds of people who need spiritual help. The *New American Standard Bible* makes this clear:

> And have mercy on some, who are doubting; save others, snatching them out of the fire; and on some have mercy with fear, hating even the garment polluted by the flesh.

THE DOUBTING (v. 22). These are the people who are wavering. They are probably the "unstable souls" Peter wrote about (2 Peter 2:14). These people are converted, but they are not grounded in the faith. Our responsibility is to have mercy on them, or show compassion toward them, by seeking to lead them away from the influences of the apostates. This kind of ministry demands a great deal of love and patience, and we must keep in mind that immature believers are like little children who think they know right from wrong. If you say no to them, they will only rebel and become more stubborn!

One of the best ways to draw them away from the false teachers is to magnify all that they have in Christ and to share His love for them in practical ways. Make their salvation so wonderful and the Word so exciting that they will lose interest in the teachings of the apostates. It is not enough merely to refute the false doctrines. There must also be a warmth of love that assures the young believer, "We care for you."

It is an open secret that false teachers prey especially on disgruntled church members. (Note verse 16—"murmurers" and "complainers.") It is important that the pastor and the people show special love and concern to new Christians and that they also minister to the mature members of the church, lest somebody stray because of neglect. Paul sent Timothy to the young believers in Thessalonica so that he might establish them in their faith (1 Thes. 2). Every young Christian needs a more mature believer to teach him how to stand and walk.

THE BURNING (v. 23a). Apparently these are the people who have left the fellowship and are now a part of the apostate group. They need to be snatched out of the fire! The angels took Lot by the hand and pulled him out of Sodom (Gen. 19:16), and sometimes that must be done in order to rescue ignorant and unstable believers from the clutches of false teachers.

There is probably a reference here to Zechariah 3:2 and also Amos 4:11. In the Zechariah passage, the "brand" was the nation Israel brought back from the Babylonian captivity and resettled in their land. God saw the people as a brand saved from the fire. In Amos 4, God was reproving the people for not heeding His warnings and judgments—poverty, poor crops, drought, pestilences, war, and even judgments like those that overthrew Sodom and Gomorrah. They were as a brand plucked out of the fire, yet they did not appreciate God's mercy.

THE DANGEROUS (v. 23b). The phrase *with fear* means "with caution." In trying to help those who have erred, we must be careful not to be trapped ourselves! Many a would-be rescuer has been drowned himself. When an unstable believer has been captured by false doctrine, we must be very careful as we try to help him, for Satan can use him to defile us. In trying to save him, we may be stained or burned ourselves!

The principle Jude was laying down was that stronger believers must never think they are beyond satanic influence. Even while serving the Lord and seeking to rescue one of His children, we can become defiled by those we want to help. The Old Testament Jews had to be very careful to avoid ceremonial defilement, and this included even their clothing (Lev. 13:47ff; 14:47; 15:17). If a "clean" person touched an "unclean" garment, then he was defiled.

We certainly must love God's people, but we must also hate sin. Wherever there is sin, Satan has a foothold and can go to work. Defilement spreads rapidly and secretly, and it must be dealt with drastically. If the Jewish priest thought that a garment was infected with leprosy, he had the garment burned.

Not every Christian is equipped to deal with false teachers or with those they have influenced and captured. It takes a good knowledge of the Word, a faithful walk with God, an understanding of Satan's devices, and certainly the fullness of the Spirit of God. It also demands spiritual discernment. It is much easier to instruct new Christians and keep them away from the false teachers than it is to snatch them out of the fire.

Commit Yourself to Jesus Christ (Jude 24-25)
This well-known benediction contains a wealth of spiritual truth for the believer to receive. If we want to keep our feet on the ground spiritually, walk straight, and not stumble, then we must yield ourselves fully to the Saviour. He alone is able to guard us, but we must "keep ourselves in the love of

God" (v. 21). He is *able* if we are *willing!*

Jude was not writing about the possibility of the believer sinning and falling from God's family. We have noted before that he made it clear in verse 1 that true believers are "preserved" and cannot be lost. He was writing about the believer's daily walk with the Lord and the danger of going astray and stumbling. If we do disobey God, we may confess our sins and receive His forgiveness (1 John 1:9). If we persist in disobedience, He will chasten us in love (Heb. 12:5-11). He will never permit one of His own to be lost.

The Father has covenanted with the Son that all of His people will one day *see* and *share* His glory (see John 17:22-24). Jesus Christ will have the special joy of presenting His bride, the church, before the Father's throne! It was the anticipation of this "joy" that helped Him endure the sufferings of the cross (Heb. 12:2). The purpose of salvation is not simply to rescue sinners from hell, as wonderful as that is. The grand purpose is that God may be glorified for all eternity (Eph. 1:6, 12, 14).

Today, there are spots and blemishes in the church, but on that day God's people shall be blameless. Satan will find nothing to accuse. The bride will be arrayed in the righteousness of Christ to the glory of God.

Knowing this, the believer has a strong motive for living for Christ and obeying His Word. We want to bring joy to His heart today as we anticipate the joy He will have when He welcomes His bride to heaven! This is the significance of 1 John 3:3—"And every man that hath this hope in him purifieth himself, even as He is pure" (cf. Eph. 5:27; Phil. 2:15).

Verse 25 is the only place in this little letter where Jude called our Lord "Saviour." Peter used this title five times. But Jude *opened* his letter by reminding his readers of "the common salvation" (v. 3) that they shared because of their faith in Jesus Christ. It is not enough to say that Jesus Christ is "*a* savior," or "*the* Saviour"; we must say that He is "*our* Saviour—*my* Saviour."

He is not only our Saviour, but He is "the only wise God." He can give you the wisdom you need to live your life to the glory of God. The false teachers boasted of their special knowledge, but they lacked spiritual wisdom. God gives wisdom to those who ask Him (James 1:5), provided they are sincerely willing to obey Him. If Christians would seek the wisdom of God in the Word of God, they would not stumble into the traps of the false teachers, but would walk to please the Lord (Col. 1:9-10).

Why should we walk in obedience to God's will? So that Christ might receive the glory!

Glory is the sum total of all that God is and all that God does. Everything about Him is glorious! The glory of man fades as the mown grass, but the glory of God goes on eternally.

Majesty means "greatness, magnificence." Only God is great. When we praise God, we praise the most magnificent Person in the universe. He is not simply King; He is King of kings! He is not simply Lord; He is Lord of lords!

Dominion has to do with God's sovereignty and rule over all things. The Greek word means "strength, might," but it carries the idea of complete control over all things.

Power means "authority," which is the right to use power. All authority belongs to Jesus Christ (Matt. 28:18), including authority over the powers of darkness (Eph. 1:19-23). As we yield to Him, we share His authority and accomplish His will.

What a magnificent doxology this is! Knowing the purpose Jude had in mind when he wrote this letter, this doxology takes on even greater significance. Jude was reminding his readers of the greatness of Jesus Christ. If only they could

catch that, they would never be led astray by false teachers. Like the young man who falls in love and marries, and is no longer interested in his old girlfriends, so the believer who keeps himself "in the love of God" (Jude 21), caught up in the glories of the Saviour, will never want to turn to Satan's substitutes.

You don't have to stumble.

If you will remember the Word, build your Christian life in faith, hope, and love, exercise spiritual discernment, and commit yourself to Christ, then He will keep you from stumbling.

Be alert!

The enemy is subtle and the dangers are great.

But the only wise God your Saviour will keep you safe and one day present you joyfully in glory!